Object Oriented Programming with C++ Lab Manual

Written by

Md. Ariful Islam

Faculty Member

Dept. of Robotics & Mechatronics Engineering

University of Dhaka, Dhaka, Bangladesh

Email: arif.rme@du.ac.bd

Educational Background:

B.Sc & M.Sc Engineering

Department of Electrical & Electronic Engineering

University of Dhaka, Bangladesh

Email: arif_eeedu@yahoo.com

1st Edition: August 2022

CONTENTS

Object Oriented Programming with C++ Lab Manual

Chap-8   **Object Oriented Programming**

CHAPTER-1: INTRODUCTION

1.1 String Input

Problem-1: Write a C++ program to get string input from user.

```cpp
#include <iostream>
#include<string>

using namespace std;

int main()
{
    string user;
    cout<<"Enter your name: ";
    cin>>user;
    cout << "Welcome "<<user<< endl;
    return 0;
}
```



```cpp
#include <iostream>
#include<string>

using namespace std;

int main()
{
    string user;
    cout<<"Enter your name: ";
    getline(cin,user);
    cout << "Welcome "<<user<< endl;
    return 0;
}
```

```cpp
#include <iostream>

using namespace std;

int main()
{
    char user [20];
    cout<<"Enter your name: ";
    cin>>user;
    cout << "Welcome "<<user<< endl;
    return 0;
}
```



```cpp
#include <iostream>
#include<stdio.h>

using namespace std;

int main()
{
    char user [20];
    cout<<"Enter your name: ";
    gets(user);
    cout << "Welcome "<<user<< endl;
    return 0;
}
```

1.2 Arithmetic Operator

Problem-2: Write a C++ program to implement arithmetic operator.

```cpp
#include <iostream>
using namespace std;
int main()
{
    int num1,num2;
    cout<<"Enter First Number: ";
    cin>>num1;
    cout<<"Enter Second Number: ";
    cin>>num2;

    //Summation
    int sum=num1+num2;
    cout<<"Summation is = "<<sum<<endl;

    //Subtraction
    int sub=num1-num2;
    cout<<"Subtraction is = "<<sub<<endl;

    //Multiplication
    int mul=num1*num2;
    cout<<"Multiplicationn is = "<<mul<<endl;

    //Division
    double div=(float)num1/num2;
    cout<<"Division is = "<<div<<endl;

    //Remainder
    int rem=num1%num2;
    cout<<"Remainder is = "<<rem<<endl;

    return 0;
}
```

```
D:\C++\LAB_C++\bin\Debug\LAB_C++.exe
Enter First Number: 10
Enter Second Number: 3
Summation is = 13
Subtraction is = 7
Multiplicationn is = 30
Division is = 3.33333
Remainder is = 1
```

1.3 Assignment Operator

Problem-3: Write a C++ program to implement Assignment operator.

```cpp
#include <iostream>
using namespace std;
int main()
{
   int x=4,y=3;

   //=
   y=x+6;
   cout<<"The result of '=' operator is: "<<y<<endl;

   //+=
   x+=5;
   cout<<"The result of '+=' operator is: "<<x<<endl;

   //-=
   x-=5;
   cout<<"The result of '-=' operator is: "<<x<<endl;

   //*=
   x*=5;
   cout<<"The result of '*=' operator is: "<<x<<endl;

   // /=
   x/=2;
   cout<<"The result of '/=' operator is: "<<x<<endl;

   // %=
   x%=3;
   cout<<"The result of '%=' operator is: "<<x<<endl;

   return 0;
}
```

```
 D:\C++\LAB_C++\bin\Debug\LAB_C++.exe
The result of '=' operator is: 10
The result of '+=' operator is: 9
The result of '-=' operator is: 4
The result of '*=' operator is: 20
The result of '/=' operator is: 10
The result of '%=' operator is: 1
```

1.4 Unary Operator

Problem-4: Write a C++ program to implement Unary operator.

```cpp
#include <iostream>

using namespace std;

int main()

{

  int x,y;

  x=4;


  //unary plus

  y=+x;

  cout<<"The result of unary plus is= "<<y<<endl;


  //unary minus

  y=-x;

  cout<<"The result of unary minus is= "<<y<<endl;


  //prefix increment

  y=++x;

  cout<<"The result of prefix increment is= "<<y<<endl;

  cout<<"The value of x is= "<<x<<endl;


  //postfix increment

  y=x++;

  cout<<"The result of postfix increment is= "<<y<<endl;
```

```cpp
cout<<"The value of x is= "<<x<<endl;


//prefix decrement

y=--x;

cout<<"The result of prefix decrement is= "<<y<<endl;

cout<<"The value of x is= "<<x<<endl;


//postfix decrement

y=x--;

cout<<"The result of postfix decrement is= "<<y<<endl;

cout<<"The value of x is= "<<x<<endl;


return 0;

}
```

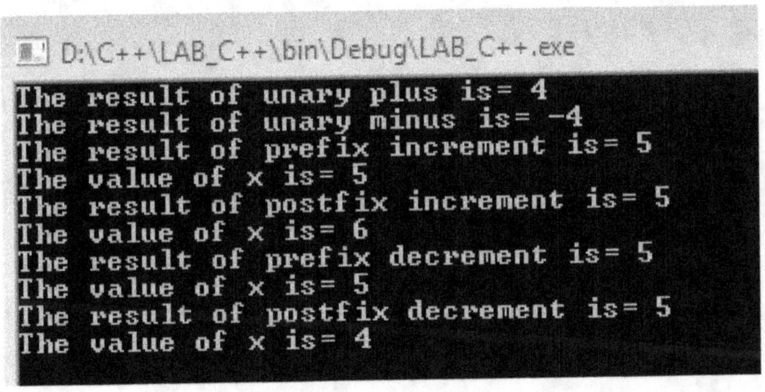

1.5 Bitwise Operator

Problem-5: Write a C++ program to implement Bitwise operator.

```cpp
#include <iostream>

using namespace std;

int main()

{

    int x,y,AND,OR,EXOR,SR,SL,NOT;

    x=8;

    y=9;


    // Bitwise AND

    AND=x&y;

    cout<<"The result of Bitwise AND is= "<<AND<<endl;


    // Bitwise OR

    OR=x|y;

    cout<<"The result of Bitwise OR is= "<<OR<<endl;


    // Bitwise EXOR

    EXOR=x^y;

    cout<<"The result of Bitwise EXOR is= "<<EXOR<<endl;


    // Bitwise Shift Right

    SR=x>>2;

    cout<<"The result of Bitwise Shift Right is= "<<SR<<endl;
```

```cpp
// Bitwise Shift Left

SL=x<<2;

cout<<"The result of Bitwise Shift Left is= "<<SL<<endl;


// Bitwise NOT

NOT=~y;

cout<<"The result of Bitwise NOT is= "<<NOT<<endl;


return 0;

}
```

```
D:\C++\LAB_C++\bin\Debug\LAB_C++.exe
The result of Bitwise AND is= 8
The result of Bitwise OR is= 9
The result of Bitwise EXOR is= 1
The result of Bitwise Shift Right is= 2
The result of Bitwise Shift Left is= 32
The result of Bitwise NOT is= -10
```

1.6 Relational Operator

Problem-6: Write C++ programs to implement Relational Operator.

6(a) Positive/ Negative Number:

```cpp
#include <iostream>
using namespace std;
int main()
{
    int num;
    cout<<"Enter your Number: ";
    cin>>num;
    if(num>0)
    {
        cout<<"Positive Number";
    }
    else if (num<0)
    {
        cout<<"Negative Number";
    }
    else
    {
        cout<<"Number is Zero";
    }
    return 0;
}
```

```
D:\C++\LAB_C++\bin\Debug\LAB_C++.exe
Enter your Number: -4
Negative Number
```

6(b) Even/Odd Number:

```cpp
#include <iostream>

using namespace std;

int main()
{
    int num;

    cout<<"Enter your Number: ";

    cin>>num;

    if(num%2==0)
    {
        cout<<"Even Number";
    }
    else
    {
        cout<<"Odd Number";
    }
    return 0;
}
```

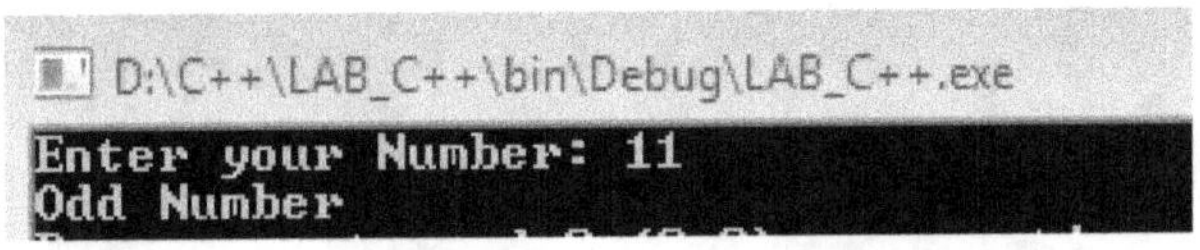

```
D:\C++\LAB_C++\bin\Debug\LAB_C++.exe
Enter your Number: 11
Odd Number
```

6(c) Large/ Small Number between two numbers:

```cpp
#include <iostream>

using namespace std;

int main()

{

   int num1,num2;

   cout<<"Enter your First Number: ";

   cin>>num1;

   cout<<"Enter your Second Number: ";

   cin>>num2;


   if(num1>num2)

   {

      cout<<"Large number is "<<num1;

   }

   else

   {

      cout<<"Large number is "<<num2;

   }

   return 0;

}
```

```
 D:\C++\LAB_C++\bin\Debug\LAB_C++.exe
Enter your First Number: 4
Enter your Second Number: 5
Large number is 5
```

6(d) Pass/Fail:

```cpp
#include <iostream>

using namespace std;

int main()
{
    int marks;
    cout<<"Enter your Marks: ";
    cin>>marks;

    if(marks>40)
    {
        cout<<"Pass";
    }
    else
    {
        cout<<"Fail";
    }
    return 0;
}
```

6(e) Absolute Value:

```cpp
#include <iostream>

using namespace std;

int main()

{

    int num, num1;

    cout<<"Enter your Value: ";

    cin>>num;


    if(num<0)

    {

        num1=-num;

        cout<<"The absolute value of your number is "<<num1;

    }

    else

    {

        cout<<"The absolute value of your number is "<<num;

    }

    return 0;

}
```

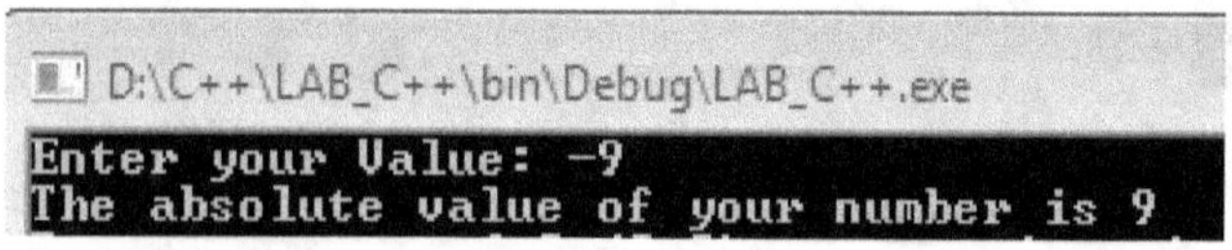

6(f) Letter Grade:

```cpp
#include <iostream>
using namespace std;
int main()
{
    int marks;
    cout<<"Enter your Marks: ";
    cin>>marks;

    if(marks>100)
    {
        cout<<"Invalid Marks!!";
    }
    else if(marks>=80)
    {
        cout<<"GPA 4";
    }
    else if(marks>=75)
    {
        cout<<"GPA 3.75";
    }
    else if(marks>=70)
    {
        cout<<"GPA 3.50";
    }
```

```cpp
else if(marks>=65)
{
    cout<<"GPA 3.25";
}
else if(marks>=60)
{
    cout<<"GPA 3";
}
else if(marks>=55)
{
    cout<<"GPA 2.75";
}
else if(marks>=50)
{
    cout<<"GPA 2.50";
}
else if(marks>=45)
{
    cout<<"GPA 2.25";
}

else if(marks>=40)
{
    cout<<"GPA 2";
}
```

```cpp
else

{

   cout<<"F";

}

return 0;

}
```

D:\C++\LAB_C++\bin\Debug\LAB_C++.exe
Enter your Marks: 50
GPA 2.50

1.7 Logical Operator

Problem-7: Write C++ programs to implement Logical Operator.

7(a) Vowel/ Consonant:

```cpp
#include <iostream>

using namespace std;

int main()

{

   char ch;

   cout<<"Enter any Letter: ";

   cin>>ch;

   if(ch=='a'||ch=='e'||ch=='i'||ch=='o'||ch=='u'||ch=='A'||ch=='E'||ch=='I'||ch=='O'||ch=='U')

   {

      cout<<"Vowel";

   }

   else

   {
```

```cpp
        cout<<"Consonant";

    }


    return 0;

}
```

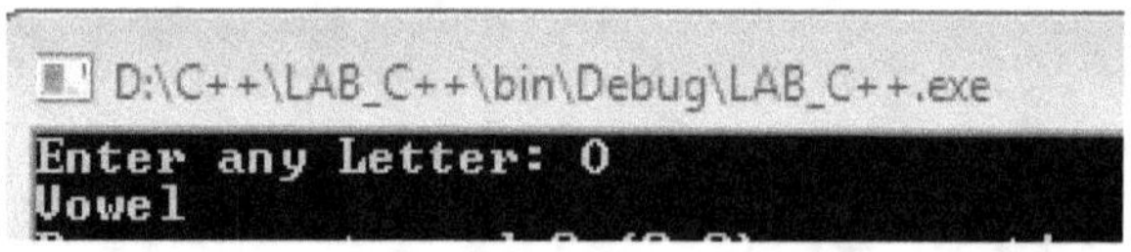

```
D:\C++\LAB_C++\bin\Debug\LAB_C++.exe
Enter any Letter: O
Vowel
```

```cpp
#include <iostream>

using namespace std;

int main()

{

    char ch;

    cout<<"Enter any Letter: ";

    cin>>ch;

    ch=tolower(ch);

    if(ch=='a'||ch=='e'||ch=='i'||ch=='o'||ch=='u')

    {

        cout<<"Vowel";

    }

    else

    {

        cout<<"Consonant";

    }

    return 0;

}
```

```
D:\C++\LAB_C++\bin\Debug\LAB_C++.exe
Enter any Letter: U
Vowel
```

7(b) Large/Small Number among three numbers:

```cpp
#include <iostream>

using namespace std;

int main()
{
    int num1,num2,num3;

    cout<<"Enter Three Numbers: ";

    cin>>num1>>num2>>num3;


    if (num1>num2 && num1>num3)
    {
        cout<<"Larger Number is "<<num1;
    }
    else if (num2>num1 && num2>num3)
    {
        cout<<"Larger Number is "<<num2;
    }
    else
    {
        cout<<"Larger Number is "<<num3;
    }
    return 0;
}
```

```
D:\C++\LAB_C++\bin\Debug\LAB_C++.exe
Enter Three Numbers: 4 6 8
Larger Number is 8
```

7(c) Leap Year:

```cpp
#include <iostream>

using namespace std;

int main()

{

    int year;

    cout<<"Enter any year: ";

    cin>>year;

    if (year%4==0 && year%100!=0)

    {

        cout<<"Leap Year";

    }

    else if (year%400==0)

    {

        cout<<"Leap Year";

    }

    else

    {

        cout<<"Not Leap Year";

    }

    return 0;

}
```

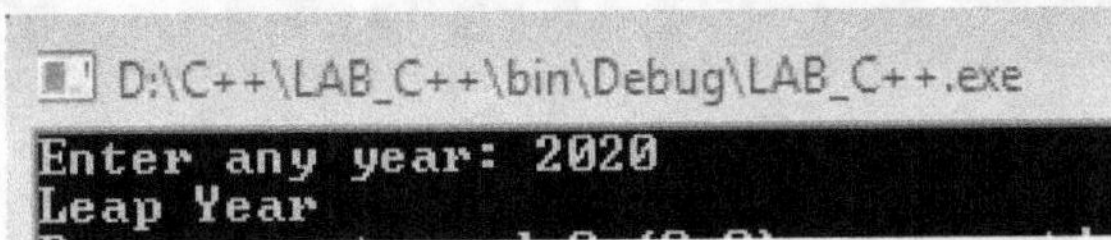

1.8 Conditional Operator

Problem-8: Write C++ programs to implement Conditional Operator.

8(a) Small/ Large Number:

#include <iostream>

using namespace std;

int main()

{

   int num1,num2,max;

   cout<<"Enter Two Numbers: ";

   cin>>num1>>num2;

   max=(num1>num2)? num1:num2;

   cout<<"Larger number is: "<<max;

   return 0;

}

8(b) Even/Odd:

```cpp
#include <iostream>

using namespace std;

int main()

{

    int num;

    cout<<"Enter any number: ";

    cin>>num;

    (num%2==0)? cout<<"Even";cout<<"Odd";

    return 0;

}
```

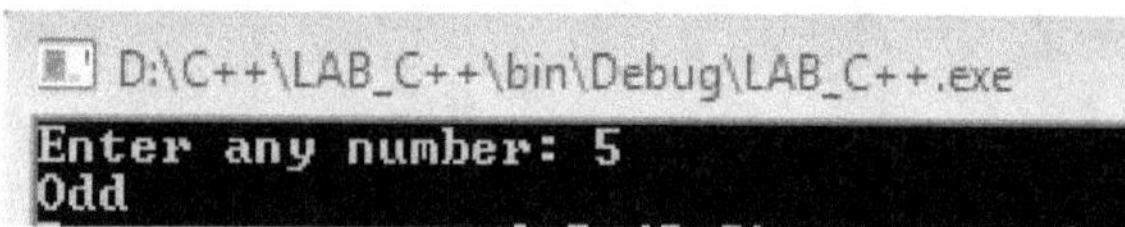

1.9 Switch

Problem-9: Write a C++ program to implement switch

9(a) Vowel/ Consonant:

```cpp
#include <iostream>

using namespace std;

int main()

{

    char ch;

    cout<<"Enter any letter: ";

    cin>>ch;
```

```cpp
switch(ch)
{
    case 'a':
    cout<<"Vowel";
    break;


    case 'e':
    cout<<"Vowel";
    break;


    case 'i':
    cout<<"Vowel";
    break;



    case 'o':
    cout<<"Vowel";
    break;


    case 'u':
    cout<<"Vowel";
    break;


    default:
    cout<<"Consonant";
```

```cpp
    }

    return 0;

}
```

D:\C++\LAB_C++\bin\Debug\LAB_C++.exe
Enter any letter: d
Consonant

```cpp
#include <iostream>

using namespace std;

int main()

{

    char ch;

    cout<<"Enter any letter: ";

    cin>>ch;


    switch(ch)

    {

        case 'a':

        case 'e':

        case 'i':

        case 'o':

        case 'u':

        cout<<"Vowel";

        break;


        default:

        cout<<"Consonant";
```

```
    }

    return 0;

}
```


1.10 Break & Continue statement

Problem-10: Write C++ programs to realize break and continue keyword.

Break:

```cpp
#include <iostream>

using namespace std;

int main()

{

   int i;

   for(i=1;i<=10;i++)

   {

     if (i==5)

     {

        break;

     }

     cout<<i<<endl;

   }

   return 0;

}
```

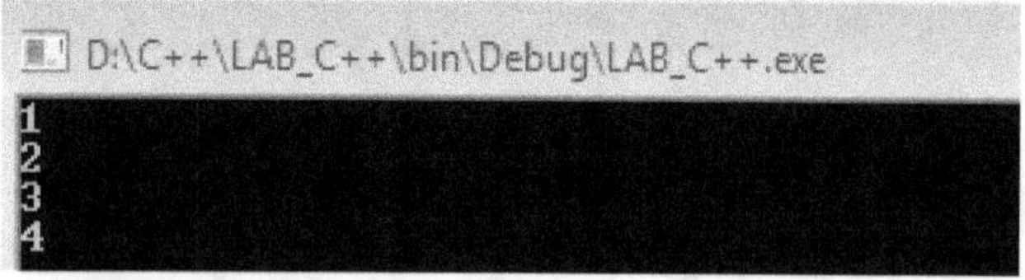

Continue:

```cpp
#include <iostream>

using namespace std;

int main()

{

    int i;

    for(i=1;i<=10;i++)

    {

        if (i==5)

        {

            continue;

        }

        cout<<i<<endl;

    }

    return 0;

}
```

CHAPTER-2: LOOP

Problem-11: Write C++ programs to realize looping or iterations.

2.1 FOR LOOP

```cpp
#include <iostream>

using namespace std;

int main()

{

    int i;

    for (i=0;i<=5;i++)

    cout << "ICT" << endl;

    return 0;

}
```


2.2 WHILE LOOP

```cpp
#include <iostream>

using namespace std;

int main()

{

    int i=0;

    while(i<=5)

    {

        cout << "ICT" << endl;
```

```cpp
        i++;

    }

    return 0;

}
```

```
D:\C++\Lab_C++\bin\Debug\Lab_C++.exe
ICT
ICT
ICT
ICT
ICT
ICT
```

2.3 DO WHILE LOOP

```cpp
#include <iostream>

using namespace std;

int main()

{

    int i=0;

    do

    {

        cout << "ICT" << endl;

        i++;

    }

    while(i<=5);

    return 0;

}
```

```
D:\C++\Lab_C++\bin\Debug\Lab_C++.exe
ICT
ICT
ICT
ICT
ICT
ICT
```

CHAPTER-3: ARRAY

3.1 1D Array

Problem-12: Write a C++ program to get user input and then print using 1D array or linear array.

```cpp
#include <iostream>

using namespace std;

int main()

{

    int mark[5];

    cin>>mark[0];

    cin>>mark[1];

    cin>>mark[2];

    cin>>mark[3];

    cin>>mark[4];

    cout << "The given marks are: "<< endl;

    cout<<mark[0]<<endl;

    cout<<mark[1]<<endl;

    cout<<mark[2]<<endl;

    cout<<mark[3]<<endl;

    cout<<mark[4]<<endl;

    return 0;

}
```

```cpp
#include <iostream>

using namespace std;

int main()

{

    int mark[5];

    for(int i=0;i<=4;i++)

    {

      cin>>mark[i];

    }

    cout<<"The given marks are: "<<endl;

    for (int i=0;i<=4;i++)

    {

      cout<<mark[i]<<endl;

    }

    return 0;

}
```

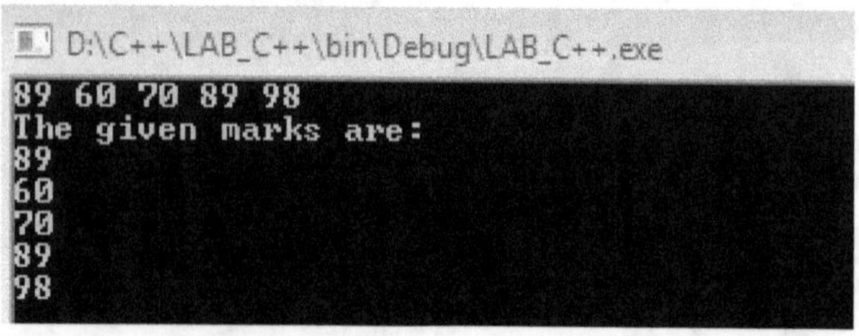

```cpp
#include <iostream>
using namespace std;
int main()
{
    int mark[5];
    for(int i=1;i<6;i++)
    {
        cout<<"Marks of student "<<i<<"=";
        cin>>mark[i];
    }
    cout<<"The given marks are: "<<endl;
    for (int i=0;i<=4;i++)
    {
        cout<<"Marks of Student"<<i<<"=";
        cout<<mark[i]<<endl;
    }
    return 0;
}
```

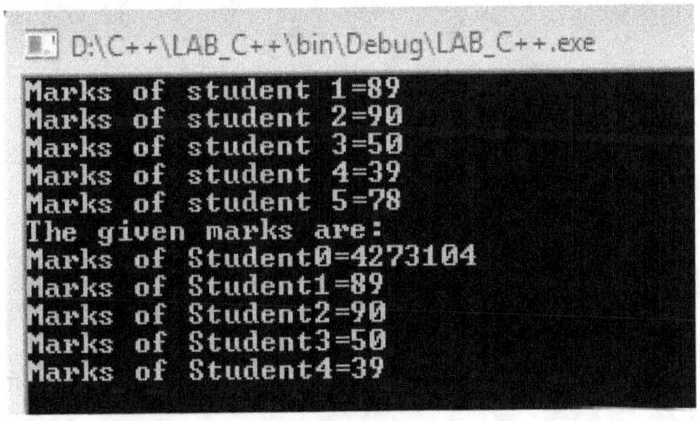

Problem-13: Write a C++ program to input the marks of students. Then calculate their total, average, maximum and minimum marks.

```cpp
#include <iostream>

using namespace std;

int main()

{

    int num,sum=0;

    cout<<"Number of Students: ";

    cin>>num;

    int students[num];

    //input

    for(int i=0;i<num;i++)

    {

        cout<<"Input the mark of student "<<i+1<<"=";

        cin>>students[i];

        sum=sum+students[i];

    }

    cout<<"Total marks are= "<<sum<<endl;

    float avg=float(sum)/num;

    cout<<"Average marks are= "<<avg<<endl;

    //maximum & minimum marks

    int max=students[0];

    for(int i=1;i<num;i++)

    {

        if(max<students[i])
```

```cpp
        {
            max=students[i];

        }

    }

    int min=students[0];

    for(int i=1;i<num;i++)

    {

        if(min>students[i])

        {

            min=students[i];

        }

    }

    cout<<"Maximum mark= "<<max<<endl;

    cout<<"Minimum mark= "<<min<<endl;

    return 0;

}
```

```
D:\C++\LAB_C++\bin\Debug\LAB_C++.exe
Number of Students: 3
Input the mark of student 1=8
Input the mark of student 2=9
Input the mark of student 3=10
Total marks are= 27
Average marks are= 9
Maximum mark= 10
Minimum mark= 8
```

3.2 2D Array

Problem-14: Write a C++ program to print the following matrix or 2D array.

```
4   5   6   7
3   4   5   6
1   2   3   4
```

```cpp
#include <iostream>

using namespace std;

int main()

{

    int matrix [3][4];

    matrix[0][0]=4;

    matrix[0][1]=5;

    matrix[0][2]=6;

    matrix[0][3]=7;

    matrix[1][0]=3;

    matrix[1][1]=4;

    matrix[1][2]=5;

    matrix[1][3]=6;

    matrix[2][0]=1;

    matrix[2][1]=2;

    matrix[2][2]=3;

    matrix[2][3]=4;

    cout<<matrix[0][0]<<" ";

    cout<<matrix[0][1]<<" ";

    cout<<matrix[0][2]<<" ";

    cout<<matrix[0][3]<<endl;;
```

```cpp
cout<<matrix[1][0]<<" ";

cout<<matrix[1][1]<<" ";

cout<<matrix[1][2]<<" ";

cout<<matrix[1][3]<<endl;

cout<<matrix[2][0]<<" ";

cout<<matrix[2][1]<<" ";

cout<<matrix[2][2]<<" ";

cout<<matrix[2][3];

return 0;

}
```

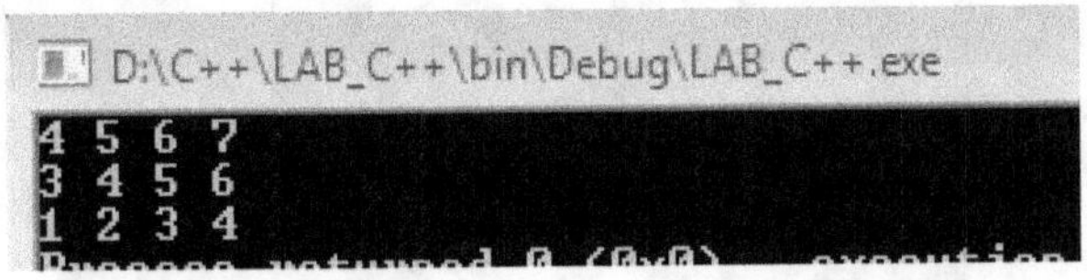

```cpp
#include <iostream>

using namespace std;

int main()

{

    int matrix [3][4]={

    {4,5,6,7},

    {3,4,5,6},

    {1,2,3,4}

    };

    cout<<matrix[0][0]<<" ";

    cout<<matrix[0][1]<<" ";

    cout<<matrix[0][2]<<" ";
```

```cpp
cout<<matrix[0][3]<<endl;;

cout<<matrix[1][0]<<" ";

cout<<matrix[1][1]<<" ";

cout<<matrix[1][2]<<" ";

cout<<matrix[1][3]<<endl;

cout<<matrix[2][0]<<" ";

cout<<matrix[2][1]<<" ";

cout<<matrix[2][2]<<" ";

cout<<matrix[2][3];

return 0;

}
```

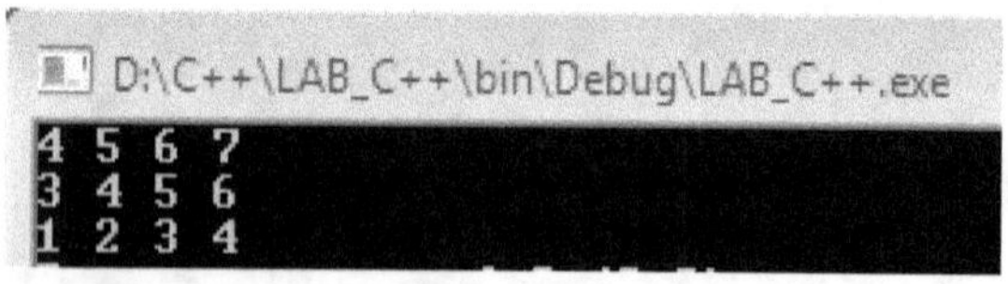

```cpp
#include <iostream>

using namespace std;

int main()

{

    int matrix [3][4]={

    {4,5,6,7},

    {3,4,5,6},

    {1,2,3,4}

    };

    for(int row=0;row<2;row++)

    {
```

```cpp
        for(int col=0;col<3;col++)

        {

            cout<<matrix[row][col]<<" ";

        }

        cout<<endl;

    }

    return 0;

}
```

```
D:\C++\LAB_C++\bin\Debug\LAB_C++.exe
4 5 6
3 4 5
```

Problem-15: Write a C++ program to get input of 2D array or matrix from user and then print the entered matrix.

```cpp
#include <iostream>

using namespace std;

int main()

{

    int matrix[2][3];

    cout<<"Enter the elements of the 2D array or matrix: "<<endl;

    for(int row=0;row<2;row++)

    {

        for(int col=0;col<3;col++)

        {

            cout<<"Enter the value of ["<<row<<"]["<<col<<"]=";

            cin>>matrix[row][col];

        }
```

```cpp
    }

    cout<<"Your 2D array or matrix is look like as: "<<endl;

    for(int row=0;row<2;row++)

    {

        for(int col=0;col<3;col++)

        {

            cout<<matrix[row][col]<<" ";

        }

        cout<<endl;

    }

    return 0;

}
```

```
D:\C++\LAB_C++\bin\Debug\LAB_C++.exe
Enter the elements of the 2D array or matrix:
Enter the value of [0][0]=1
Enter the value of [0][1]=2
Enter the value of [0][2]=3
Enter the value of [1][0]=4
Enter the value of [1][1]=5
Enter the value of [1][2]=6
Your 2D array or matrix is look like as:
1 2 3
4 5 6
```

CHAPTER-4: POINTER

4.1 Address in C++

***Problem-16:** Write a C++ program to get the address of three variables using reference operator.*

```cpp
#include <iostream>

using namespace std;

int main()

{

    int num1,num2,num3;

    cout<<"Enter three numbers: ";

    cin>>num1>>num2>>num3;


    cout<<"The address of number 1 is: ";

    cout << &num1 << endl;


    cout<<"The address of number 2 is: ";

    cout << &num2 << endl;


    cout<<"The address of number 3 is: ";

    cout << &num3 << endl;

    return 0;

}
```

4.2 Reference & Dereference Operator

Problem-17: Write a C++ Program to demonstrate the working of pointer using reference (&) and dereference (*) operator.

```cpp
#include <iostream>

using namespace std;

int main()

{

    int x;

    int *p;

    cout<<"Enter any value: ";

    cin>>x;

    p=&x;


    cout<<x<<endl;

    cout<<&x<<endl;

    cout<<p<<endl;

    cout<<*p<<endl;

    return 0;

}
```

```
D:\C++\LAB_C++\bin\Debug\LAB_C++.exe
Enter any value: 5
5
0x22ff18
0x22ff18
5
```

```cpp
#include <iostream>

using namespace std;

int main()

{

    int *pc, c;


    c = 5;
    cout << "Address of c (&c): " << &c << endl;
    cout << "Value of c (c): " << c << endl << endl;


    pc = &c;    // Pointer pc holds the memory address of variable c
    cout << "Address that pointer pc holds (pc): "<< pc << endl;
    cout << "Content of the address pointer pc holds (*pc): " << *pc << endl << endl;


    c = 11;    // The content inside memory address &c is changed from 5 to 11.
    cout << "Address pointer pc holds (pc): " << pc << endl;
    cout << "Content of the address pointer pc holds (*pc): " << *pc << endl << endl;


    *pc = 2;
    cout << "Address of c (&c): " << &c << endl;
    cout << "Value of c (c): " << c << endl << endl;
    return 0;

}
```

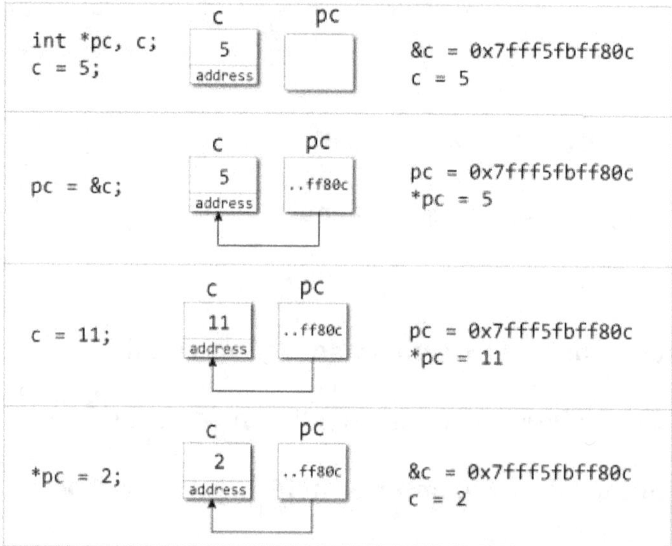

Explanation of program

- When c = 5; the value 5 is stored in the address of variable c - 0x7fff5fbff8c.
- When pc = &c; the pointer pc holds the address of c - 0x7fff5fbff8c, and the expression (dereference operator) *pc outputs the value stored in that address, 5.
- When c = 11; since the address pointer pc holds is the same as c - 0x7fff5fbff8c, change in the value of c is also reflected when the expression *pc is executed, which now outputs 11.
- When *pc = 2; it changes the content of the address stored by pc - 0x7fff5fbff8c. This is changed from 11 to 2. So, when we print the value of c, the value is 2 as well.

Common mistakes when working with pointers

- Suppose, you want pointer pc to point to the address of c. Then,
- int c, *pc;
- pc=c; /* Wrong! pc is address whereas, c is not an address. */
- *pc=&c; /* Wrong! *pc is the value pointed by address whereas, &c is an address. */
- pc=&c; /* Correct! pc is an address and, &pc is also an address. */
- *pc=c; /* Correct! *pc is the value pointed by address and, c is also a value. */

4.3 Summation using pointer

Problem-18: Write a C++ program to add two numbers using pointer

```cpp
#include <iostream>

using namespace std;

int main()
{
    int num1,num2;

    cout<<"Enter two numbers: ";

    cin>>num1>>num2;


    int *p1=&num1;

    int *p2=&num2;


    int sum=*p1+*p2;

    cout<<"Summation is: "<<sum;

    return 0;
}
```

4.4 Arrays of Pointer

Problem-19: Write a C++ program to access the arrays of pointers.

```cpp
#include <iostream>

using namespace std;

int main()

{

    int a[3]={10,20,30};

    int *p[3],i;

    for(int i=0;i<3;i++)

    {

      p[i]=&a[i];

    }

    cout << "The values of arrays are: " << endl;

    for(int i=0;i<3;i++)

    {

      cout<<*p[i]<<endl;

    }

    cout << "The addresses of arrays are: " << endl;

    for(int i=0;i<3;i++)

    {

      cout<<&p[i]<<endl;

    }

    return 0;

}
```

```
D:\C++\LAB_C++\bin\Debug\LAB_C++.exe
The values of arrays are:
10
20
30
The addresses of arrays are:
0x22fee8
0x22feec
0x22fef0
```

CHAPTER-5: FUNCTIONS

5.1 Arithmetic operation using function

Problem-20: Write a C++ program to implement arithmetic operation by creating multiple functions.

```cpp
#include <iostream>

using namespace std;

void summation(int a, int b)
{
    int sum=a+b;
    cout<<"Summation is: "<<sum<<endl;
}

void subtraction(int a, int b)
{
    int sub=a-b;
    cout<<"subtraction is: "<<sub<<endl;
}

void multiplication(int a, int b)
{
    int mul=a+b;
    cout<<"Multiplication is: "<<mul<<endl;
}
```

```cpp
void division(int a, int b)

{

    float div=(float)a/b;

    cout<<"Division is: "<<div<<endl;

}

int main()

{

    int a,b;

    cout<<"Enter two numbers: ";

    cin>>a>>b;

    summation(a,b);

    subtraction(a,b);

    multiplication(a,b);

    division(a,b);

    return 0;

}
```

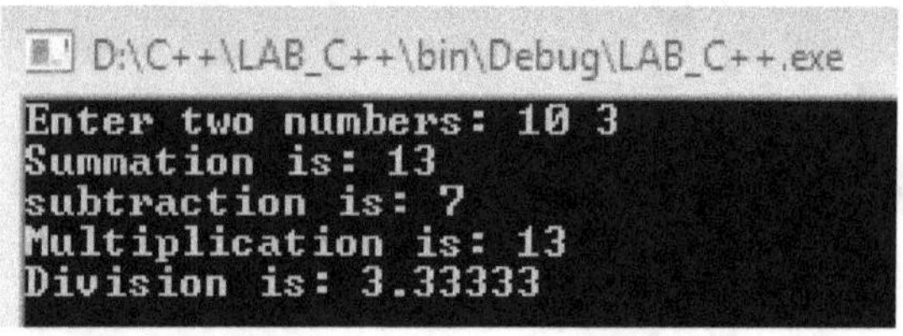

5.2 Random Number Generation

Problem-21(a): Write a C++ program to generate a random number.

```cpp
#include<iostream>
#include<stdlib.h>
using namespace std;
int main()
{
    int random_number= rand();
    cout<<"Random Number: "<<random_number<<endl;
    return 0;
}
```

```
D:\C++\LAB_C++\bin\Debug\LAB_C++.exe
Random Number: 41
```

Problem-21(b): Write a C++ program to generate 5 random numbers.

```cpp
#include<iostream>
#include<stdlib.h>
using namespace std;
int main()
{
    for(int i=0;i<5;i++)
    {
        int random_number= rand();
        cout<<"Random Number: "<<random_number<<endl;
    }
    return 0;
```

```
}
```

```
D:\C++\LAB_C++\bin\Debug\LAB_C++.exe
Random Number: 41
Random Number: 18467
Random Number: 6334
Random Number: 26500
Random Number: 19169
```

Problem-21(c): Write a C++ program to generate random numbers between 1 and 5.

```cpp
#include<iostream>

#include<stdlib.h>

using namespace std;

int main()

{

   for(int i=0;i<5;i++)

   {

    int random_number= rand()%5;

    cout<<"Random Number: "<<random_number<<endl;

   }

   return 0;

}
```

```
D:\C++\LAB_C++\bin\Debug\LAB_C++.exe
Random Number: 1
Random Number: 2
Random Number: 4
Random Number: 0
Random Number: 4
```

```cpp
#include<iostream>

#include<stdlib.h>

using namespace std;
```

```cpp
int main()

{

  for(int i=0;i<5;i++)

  {

    int random_number= rand()%5+1;

    cout<<"Random Number: "<<random_number<<endl;

  }

  return 0;

}
```


5.3 Guess Game

Problem-22: Write a C++ program to implement a guessing game. User will be asked to submit his or her guess number. If the guess number is equal to the generated random number, then congratulate him or her; otherwise tell the right number.

```cpp
#include<iostream>

#include<stdlib.h>

using namespace std;

int main()

{

  int guess_number,random_number;

  cout<<"Enter your guess number between 1 and 3"<<endl;

  cin>>guess_number;
```

```cpp
    random_number=rand()%3+1;

    if(guess_number==random_number)

    {

        cout<<"You have won"<<endl;

    }

    else

    {

        cout<<"You have lost!Try again!"<<endl;

        cout<<"Random number was: "<<random_number<<endl;

    }

    return 0;

}
```

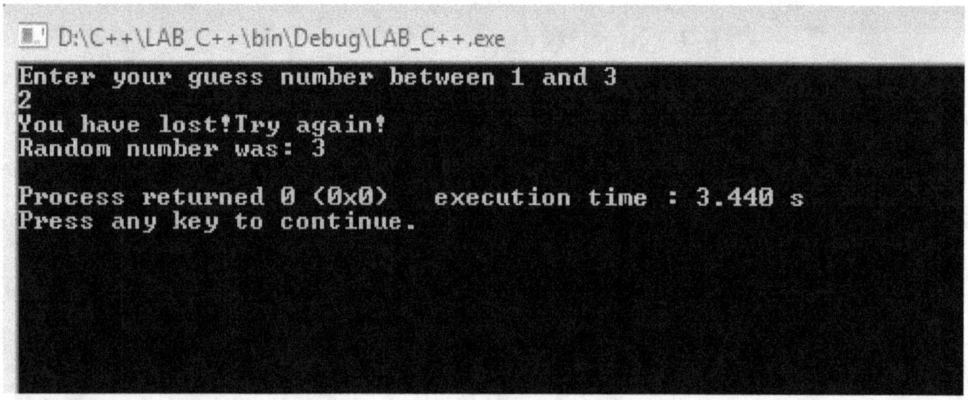

```
D:\C++\LAB_C++\bin\Debug\LAB_C++.exe

Enter your guess number between 1 and 3
2
You have lost!Try again!
Random number was: 3

Process returned 0 (0x0)   execution time : 3.440 s
Press any key to continue.
```

```cpp
#include<iostream>

#include<stdlib.h>

using namespace std;

int main()

{

    while(1)

    {
```

```cpp
int guess_number,random_number;

cout<<"Enter your guess number between 1 and 3"<<endl;

cin>>guess_number;

random_number=rand()%3+1;

if(guess_number==random_number)

{

   cout<<"You have won"<<endl;

}

else

{

   cout<<"You have lost!Try again!"<<endl;

   cout<<"Random number was: "<<random_number<<endl;

}

}

   return 0;

}
```

```
D:\C++\LAB_C++\bin\Debug\LAB_C++.exe

Enter your guess number between 1 and 3
2
You have lost!Try again!
Random number was: 3
Enter your guess number between 1 and 3
1
You have lost!Try again!
Random number was: 3
Enter your guess number between 1 and 3
3
You have lost!Try again!
Random number was: 2
Enter your guess number between 1 and 3
3
You have lost!Try again!
Random number was: 2
Enter your guess number between 1 and 3
1
You have lost!Try again!
Random number was: 3
Enter your guess number between 1 and 3
2
You have won
Enter your guess number between 1 and 3
```

5.4 Function Overloading

Problem-23: Write a C++ program to realize the function overloading.

```cpp
#include<iostream>

using namespace std;

void sum(int a,int b)

{

    int sum=a+b;

    cout<<"Your sum is: "<<sum<<endl;

}

void sum(int a,int b,int c)

{

    int sum=a+b+c;

    cout<<"Your sum is: "<<sum<<endl;

}

int main()
```

```cpp
{

    sum(20,30);

    sum(20,30,40);

    return 0;

}
```

```
D:\C++\LAB_C++\bin\Debug\LAB_C++.exe
Your sum is: 50
Your sum is: 90
```

5.5 Passing arrays and arguments into function

Problem-24(a): Write a C++ program to pass an array into a function.

```cpp
#include<iostream>

using namespace std;

void display_array(int num[],int size)

{

    for(int i=0;i<=4;i++)

    {

        cout<<"Inside the function: "<<num[i]<<endl;

    }

}

int main()

{

    int number[5]={10,20,30,40,50};

    display_array(number,5);

    return 0;

}
```

```
D:\C++\LAB_C++\bin\Debug\LAB_C++.exe
Inside the function: 10
Inside the function: 20
Inside the function: 30
Inside the function: 40
Inside the function: 50
```

Problem-24(b): Write a C++ program to pass argument by value into a function.

```cpp
#include<iostream>

using namespace std;

void display(int num)

{

    num=20;

}

int main()

{

    int x=10;

    cout<<"Before calling the function x= "<<x<<endl;

    display(x);

    cout<<"After calling the function x= "<<x<<endl;

    return 0;

}
```

```
D:\C++\LAB_C++\bin\Debug\LAB_C++.exe
Before calling the function x= 10
After calling the function x= 10
```

Problem-24(c): Write a C++ program to pass argument by reference into a function.

```cpp
#include<iostream>

using namespace std;

void display(int *num)

{

   *num=20;

}

int main()

{

   int x=10;

   cout<<"Before calling the function x= "<<x<<endl;

   display(&x);

   cout<<"After calling the function x= "<<x<<endl;

   return 0;

}
```

5.6 Recursion

Problem-25: Write a C++ program to find the factorial of a number.

```cpp
#include<iostream>
using namespace std;
int fact(int n)
{
    if(n==1)
    {
        return 1;
    }
    else
    {
        return n*fact(n-1);
    }
}
int main()
{
    int a;
    cout<<"Enter your number you want to find the factorial: ";
    cin>>a;
    int factorial=fact(a);
    cout<<"The factorial of "<<a<<" is: "<<factorial<<endl;
    return 0;
}
```

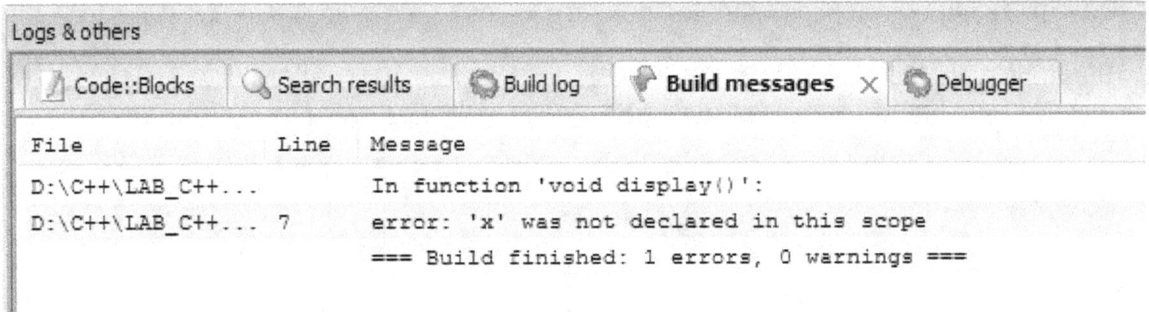

5.7 Local & Global Variable

Problem-26: Write a C++ program to realize the Local & Global variable.

```cpp
#include<iostream>

using namespace std;

void display()

{

    cout<<"Inside the display function x= "<<x<<endl;

}

int main()

{

    int x=10;//local variable

    cout<<"Inside the main function x= "<<x<<endl;

    return 0;

}
```



```cpp
#include<iostream>

using namespace std;
```

```cpp
int x=10;//global variable

void display()

{

    cout<<"Inside the display function x= "<<x<<endl;

}

int main()

{

    cout<<"Inside the main function x= "<<x<<endl;

    display();

    return 0;

}
```

```
D:\C++\LAB_C++\bin\Debug\LAB_C++.exe
Inside the main function x= 10
Inside the display function x= 10
```

5.8 Scope Resolution Operator

Problem-27(a): Write a C++ program to skip the global variable and then print the local variable remaining within the main function.

```cpp
#include<iostream>

using namespace std;

int x=10;//global variable

int main()

{

    int x=50;//local variable

    cout<<"x= "<<x<<endl;

    return 0;

}
```

Problem-27(b): Write a C++ program to print the global variable remaining within the main function using scope resolution operator.

```cpp
#include<iostream>

using namespace std;

int x=10;//global variable

int main()

{

    int x=50;//local variable

    cout<<"x= "<<::x<<endl;

    return 0;

}
```


Problem-27(c): Write a C++ program to change the value of global variable remaining within the main function using scope resolution operator.

```cpp
#include<iostream>

using namespace std;

int x=10;//global variable

int main()

{

    int x=50;//local variable

    ::x=20;

    cout<<"x= "<<::x<<endl;
```

```
    return 0;

}
```

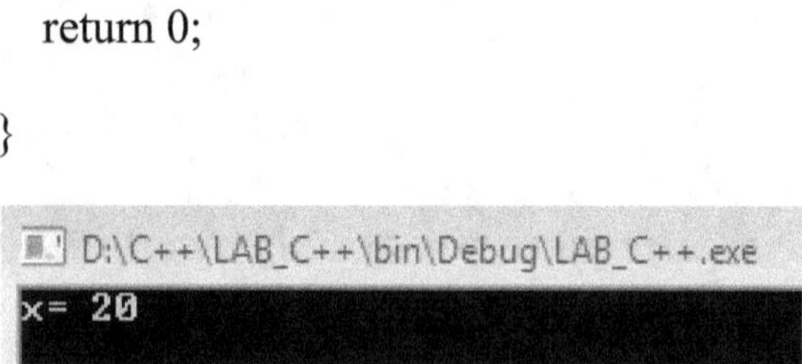

5.9 Function Template

Problem-28(a): Write a C++ program to create a function template to perform addition of two integer or float numbers (the two are same parameter).

int type sum	float type sum

<pre>#include <iostream>
#include<conio.h>
using namespace std;
template<class MyTemplate>
MyTemplate add (MyTemplate a, MyTemplate b)
{
   return a+b;
}
int main()
{
   int a=20;
   int b=2;
   cout<<"Integer type sum is: "<<add(a,b);
   getch();
}</pre>
	<pre>#include <iostream>
	#include<conio.h>
	using namespace std;
	template<class MyTemplate>
	MyTemplate add (MyTemplate a, MyTemplate b)
	{
	   return a+b;
	}
	int main()
	{
	   float a=20.5;
	   float b=2.5;
	   cout<<"Float type sum is: "<<add(a,b);
	   getch();
	}</pre>

D:\C++\FT\bin\Debug\FT.exe Integer type sum is: 22	D:\C++\FT\bin\Debug\FT.exe Float type sum is: 23

Problem-28(b): Write a C++ program to create a function template to perform addition of multiple parameters (mixture of integer and float numbers).

```
#include <iostream>

#include<conio.h>

using namespace std;

template<class MyTemplate1, class MyTemplate2>
```

```cpp
MyTemplate1 add (MyTemplate1 a, MyTemplate2 b)
{
    return a+b;
}
int main()
{
    int a=20;
    float b=2.5;
    cout<<"Any type sum is: "<<add(a,b);
    getch();
}
```

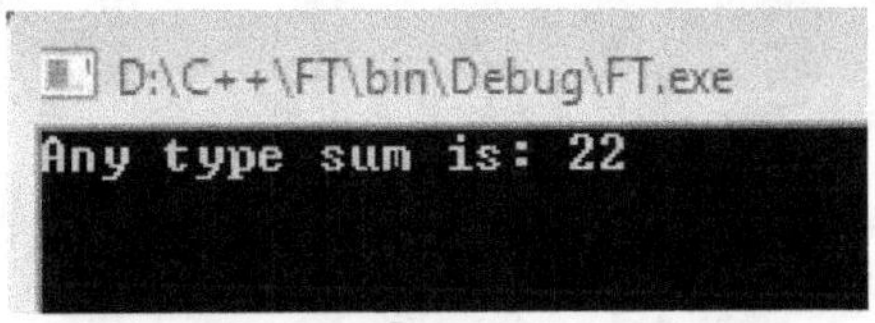

```
D:\C++\FT\bin\Debug\FT.exe
Any type sum is: 22
```

```cpp
#include <iostream>
#include<conio.h>
using namespace std;
template<class MyTemplate1, class MyTemplate2>
MyTemplate2 add (MyTemplate1 a, MyTemplate2 b)
{
    return a+b;
}
int main()
{
    int a=20;
```

```
float b=2.5;

cout<<"Any type sum is: "<<add(a,b);

getch();
}
```


CHAPTER-6: STRING

6.1 String library function

Problem-29: Write a C++ program to realize the string library function.

```cpp
#include<iostream>

#include<cstring>

using namespace std;

int main()
{
    //strlen()

    char name[]="Comilla";

    int len=strlen(name);

    cout<<"Length is: "<<len<<endl;


    //strcpy()

    char name1[]="Comilla";

    char name2[10];

    strcpy(name2,name1);
```

```cpp
cout<<"The copied string which is stored in name2 variable is: "<<name2<<endl;


//strcat()

char name3[]="Comilla";

char name4[]="University";

strcat(name3,name4);

cout<<"String Concatination is: "<<name3<<endl;


//strupr()

char name5[]="Comilla";

strupr(name5);

cout<<"Uper case is: "<<name5<<endl;


//strlwr()

char name6[]="COMILLA";

strlwr(name6);

cout<<"Lower case is: "<<name6<<endl;


//strcmp()

char name7[]="Comilla";

char name8[]="Cumilla";

int value=strcmp(name7,name8);

if(value==0)

{

    cout<<"Strings are equal";
```

```cpp
}
else
{
    cout<<"Strings are not equal";
}
return 0;
}
```

```
D:\C++\LAB_C++\bin\Debug\LAB_C++.exe
Length is: 7
The copied string which is stored in name2 variable is: Comilla
String Concatination is: ComillaUniversity
Uper case is: COMILLA
Lower case is: comilla
Strings are not equal
```

CHAPTER-7: FILE

7.1 Create a file

Problem-30(a): Write a C++ program to create a file.

```cpp
#include<iostream>
#include<fstream>
using namespace std;
int main()
{
    ofstream dept;
    dept.open("ict_department.txt");
    dept<<"Department of Information & Communication Technology which is under the faculty of engineering at Comilla University.";
    dept.close();
    return 0;
}
```

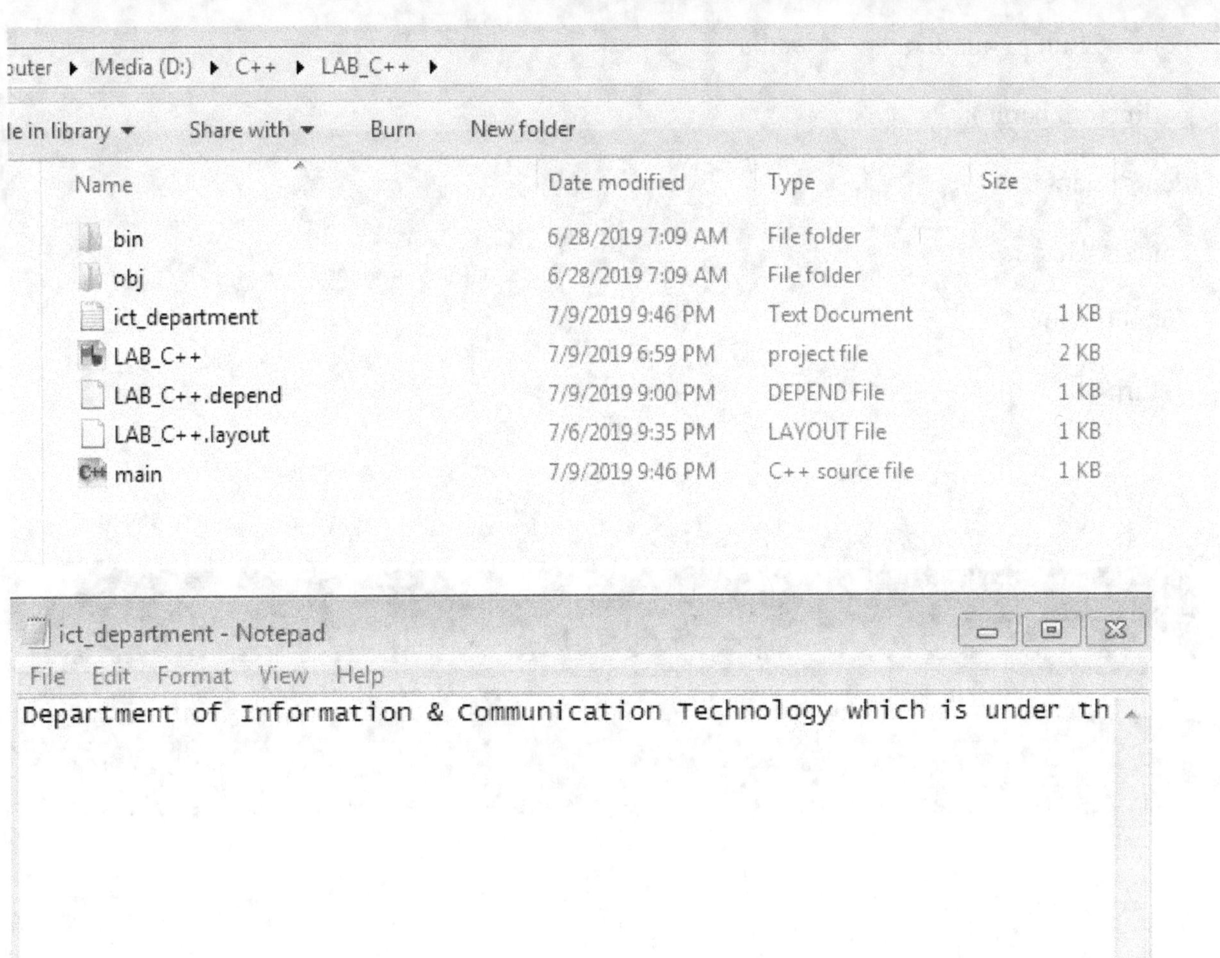

Problem-30(b): Write a C++ program to create a file from user input.

```cpp
#include<iostream>

#include<fstream>

#include<string>

using namespace std;

int main()

{

  string name;

  ofstream dept;

  dept.open("ict_department.txt");
```

```cpp
cout<<"Enter your details: "<<endl;

getline(cin,name);

dept<<name;

cout<<"Data is stored."<<endl;

dept.close();

 return 0;

}
```

```
D:\C++\LAB_C++\bin\Debug\LAB_C++.exe
Enter your details:
I am a second year student of ICT department at the comilla university.
Data is stored.
```

```
ict_department - Notepad
File  Edit  Format  View  Help
I am a second year student of ICT department at the comilla university
```

7.2 Read data from file

Problem-30(c): Write a C++ program to read data from a file.

```cpp
#include<iostream>

#include<fstream>

#include<string>

using namespace std;

int main()

{

  string line;

  ifstream dept("ict_department.txt");
```

```cpp
    while(getline(dept,line))

    {

       cout<<line<<endl;

    }

    dept.close();

     return 0;

}
```

```
D:\C++\LAB_C++\bin\Debug\LAB_C++.exe
I am a second year student of ICT department at the comilla university.

Process returned 0 (0x0)    execution time : 0.770 s
Press any key to continue.
```

Problem-29(d): Write a C++ program to write three student's name, department and university provided by user into a file.

```cpp
#include <iostream>

#include<fstream>

#include<string>

using namespace std;

int main()

{

    string name,dept,univ;

    ofstream std_details;

    std_details.open("student details.txt",ios::out|ios::app);

    for(int i=1;i<=3;i++)

    {

        cout<<"Enter the name of student "<<i<<" ="<<endl;

        getline(cin,name);
```

```cpp
        std_details<<name<<"\t";

        cout<<"Enter the name of his department= "<<endl;

        getline(cin,dept);

        std_details<<dept<<"\t";

        cout<<"Enter the name of his university= "<<endl;

        getline(cin,univ);

        std_details<<univ<<"\t"<<endl;

    }

    std_details.close();

    return 0;

}
```

student details - Notepad

File   Edit   Format   View   Help

```
ARIF    EEE    DU
ABID    CSE    JU
Asif    ICT    BUET
```

CHAPTER-8: OBJECT ORIENTED PROGRAMMING

8.1 Class & Object

Problem-31: Write a C++ program to create class named 'student' and two objects named 'rahim' & 'karim' respectively. Then use that class to print ID and GPA of rahim & karim.

```cpp
#include <iostream>

#include<conio.h>

using namespace std;

class student

{

    public:

    int id;

    double gpa;

};

int main()

{

    student rahim, karim;

    rahim.id=101;

    rahim.gpa=3.97;

    cout << rahim.id<<" "<<rahim.gpa<<endl;


    karim.id=102;

    karim.gpa=3.99;

    cout << karim.id<<" "<<karim.gpa<<endl;

    getch();
```

```
}
```

```
D:\C++\LAB_C++\bin\Debug\LAB_C++.exe
101 3.97
102 3.99
```

8.2 Adding function within class

Problem-32: Write a C++ program to add a function named 'display' inside the 'student' class and then call 'display' function within the main function to print ID and GPA of two students named 'rahim' and 'karim' respectively.

```cpp
#include <iostream>

#include<conio.h>

using namespace std;

class student

{

    public:

    int id;

    double gpa;

    void display()

    {

        cout<<id<<" "<<gpa<<endl;

    }

};

int main()

{

    student rahim, karim;

    rahim.id=101;
```

```cpp
    rahim.gpa=3.97;

    rahim.display();


    karim.id=102;

    karim.gpa=3.99;

    karim.display();

    getch();

}
```


Problem-33: Write a C++ program to add a parametrized function named 'setValue' inside the 'student' class to set the ID and GPA of two students named 'rahim' & 'karim' respectively. Also print those values by creating a function named 'display' inside that class.

```cpp
#include <iostream>

#include<conio.h>

using namespace std;

class student

{

  public:

  int id;

  double gpa;

  void display()

  {
```

```cpp
        cout<<id<<" "<<gpa<<endl;

    }

    void setValue(int x,double y)

    {

        id=x;

        gpa=y;

    }

};

int main()

{

    student rahim, karim;

    rahim.setValue(101,3.97);

    rahim.display();


    karim.setValue(102,3.99);

    karim.display();

    getch();

}
```

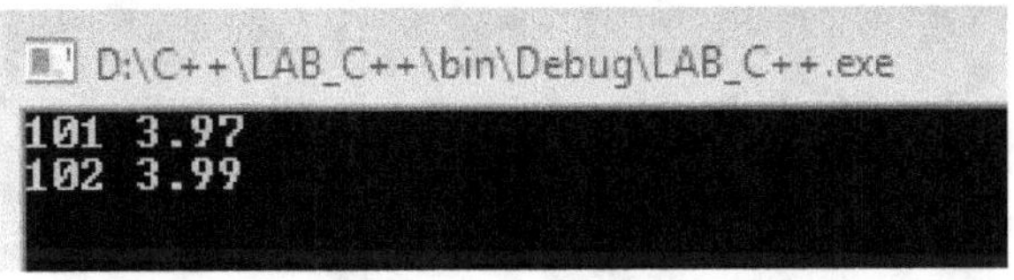

8.3 Constructor

Problem-34: Write a C++ program to initialize object using parametrized constructor.

```cpp
#include <iostream>

#include<conio.h>

using namespace std;

class student

{

    public:

    int id;

    double gpa;

    void display()

    {

        cout<<id<<" "<<gpa<<endl;

    }

    student(int x,double y)

    {

        id=x;

        gpa=y;

    }

};

int main()

{

    student rahim(101,3.97);

    rahim.display();
```

```
    student karim(102,3.99);

    karim.display();

    getch();

}
```

```
D:\C++\LAB_C++\bin\Debug\LAB_C++.exe
101 3.97
102 3.99
```

Problem-35: Write a C++ program to realize default constructor.

```cpp
#include <iostream>

#include<conio.h>

using namespace std;

class student

{

    public:

    int id;

    double gpa;

    void display()

    {

        cout<<id<<" "<<gpa<<endl;

    }

    student(int x,double y)

    {

        id=x;

        gpa=y;
```

```cpp
    }
    student()
    {
        cout<<"Default constructor is called"<<endl;
    }
};
int main()
{
    student jamal;
    student rahim(101,3.97);
    rahim.display();

    student karim(102,3.99);
    karim.display();
    getch();
}
```

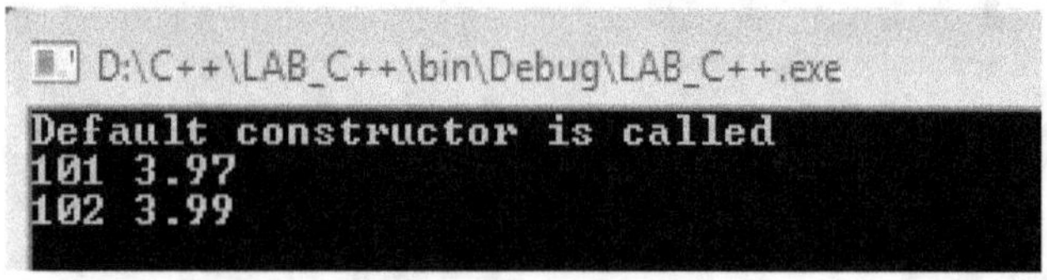

8.4 Destructor

Problem-36: Write a C++ program to realize destructor.

```cpp
#include <iostream>

using namespace std;

class ICT

{

    public:

        ICT () //constructor defined

        {

            cout << "Hey look I am in constructor" << endl;

        }

        ~ICT() //destructor defined

        {

            cout << "Hey look I am in destructor" << endl;

        }

};


int main()

{

    ICT c; //constructor is called

    cout << "function main is terminating...." << endl;

    /*....object c goes out of scope ,now destructor is being called...*/

    return 0;

} //end of program
```

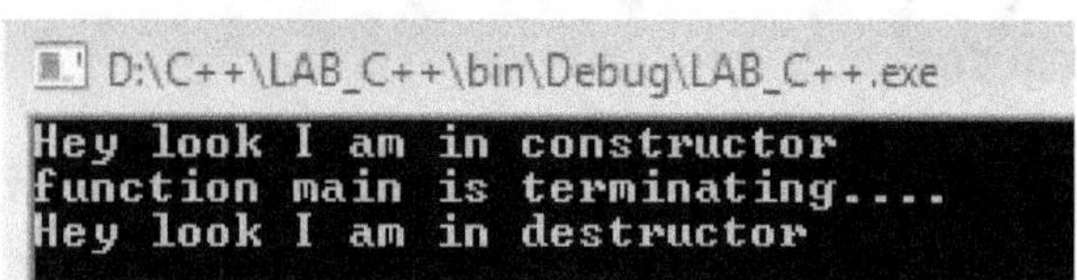

8.5 Separate file for classes

Problem-37(a): How to open separate files for class?

Follow the following steps

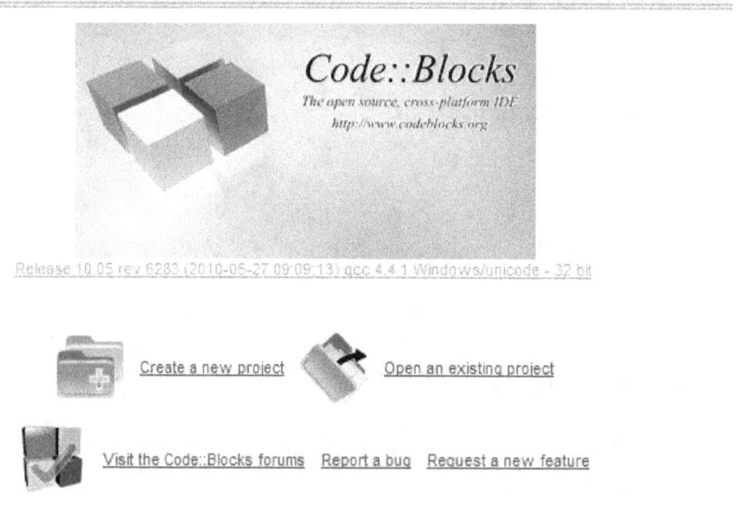

Click on 'Create a new project'

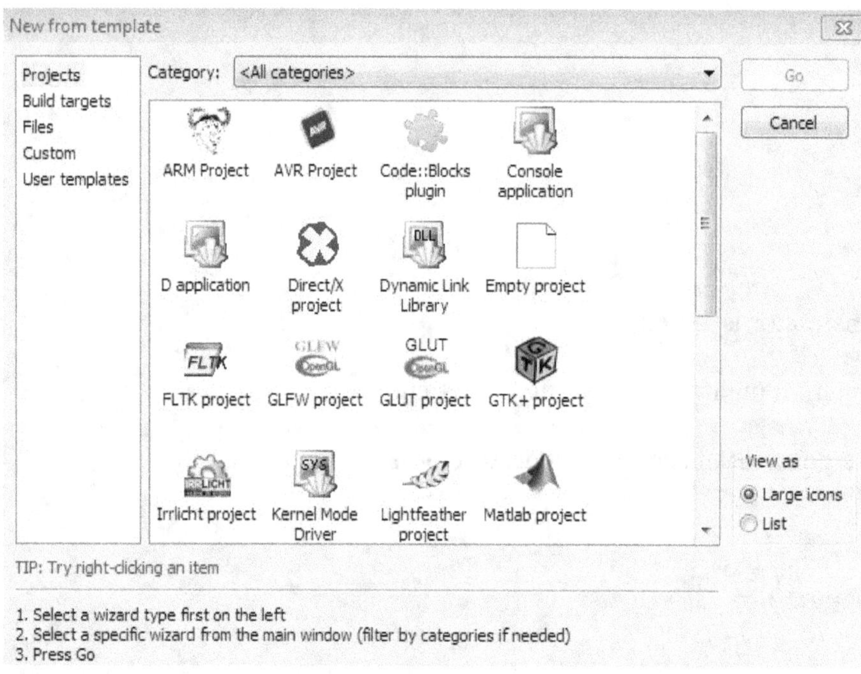

Select 'Console application' and click on 'go' option

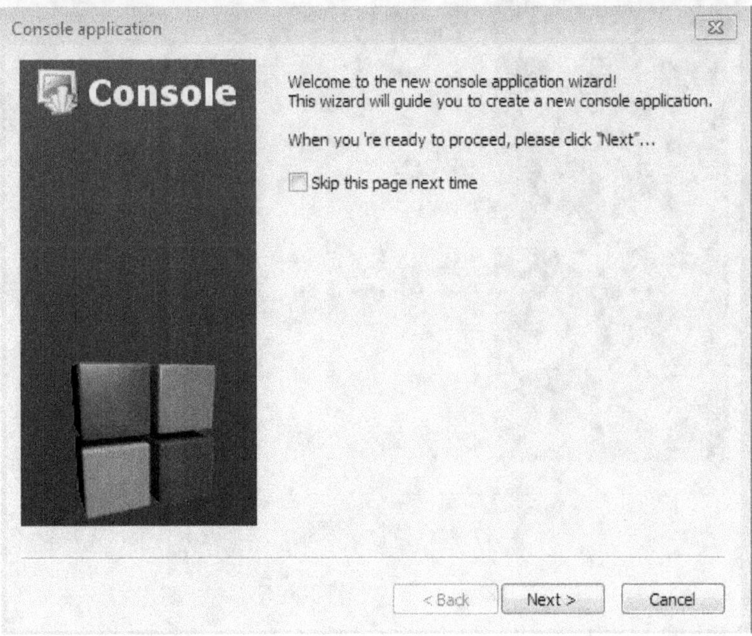

Click 'next'

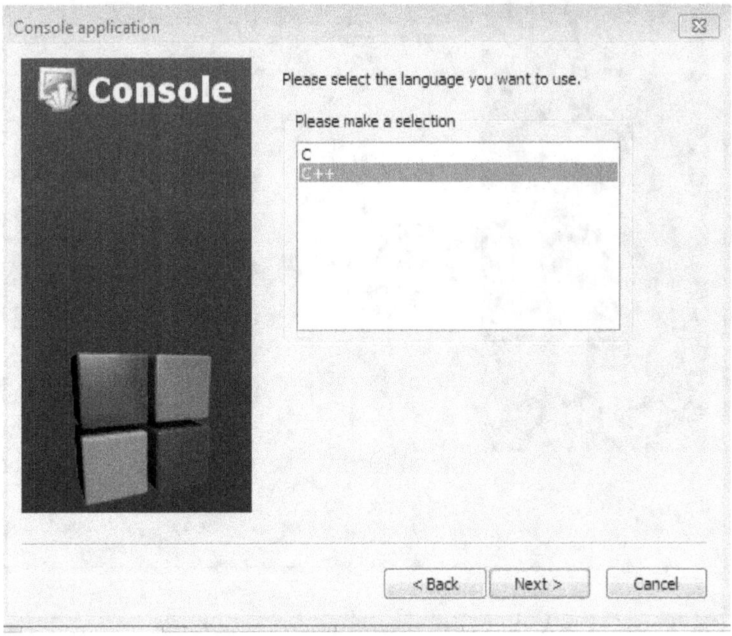

Choose C++ and click 'next'

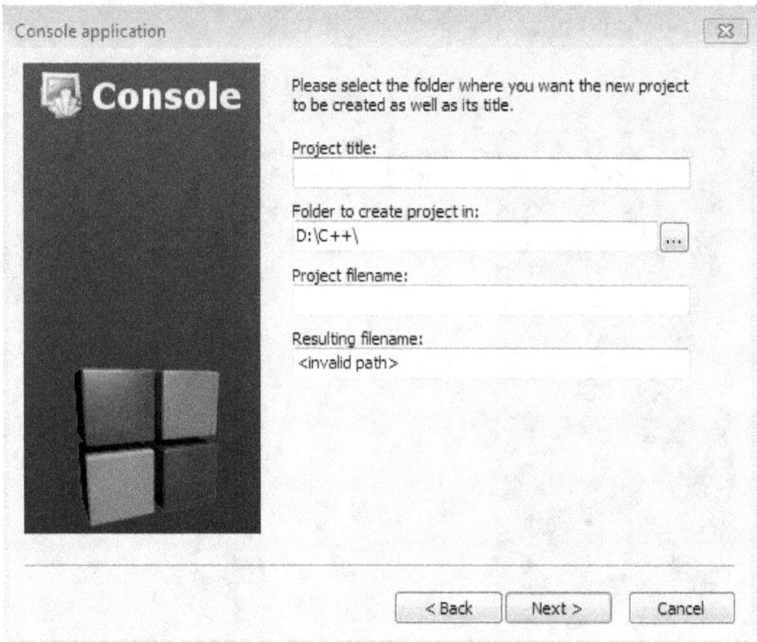

Write anything as a project title

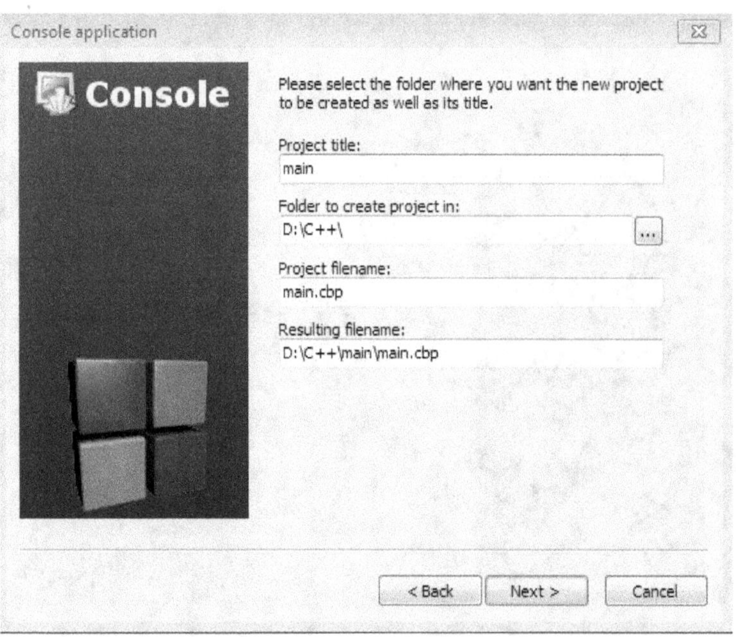

I write main as a project title, then click 'next'

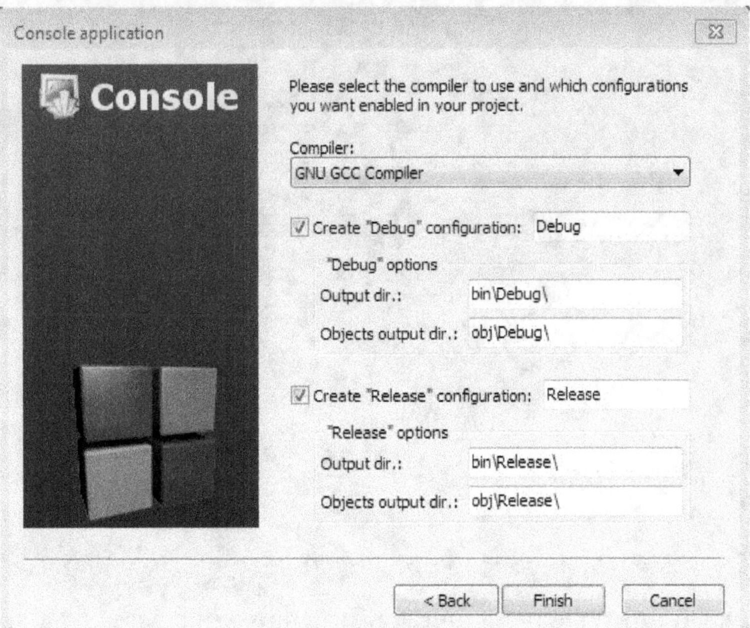

Click 'finish'

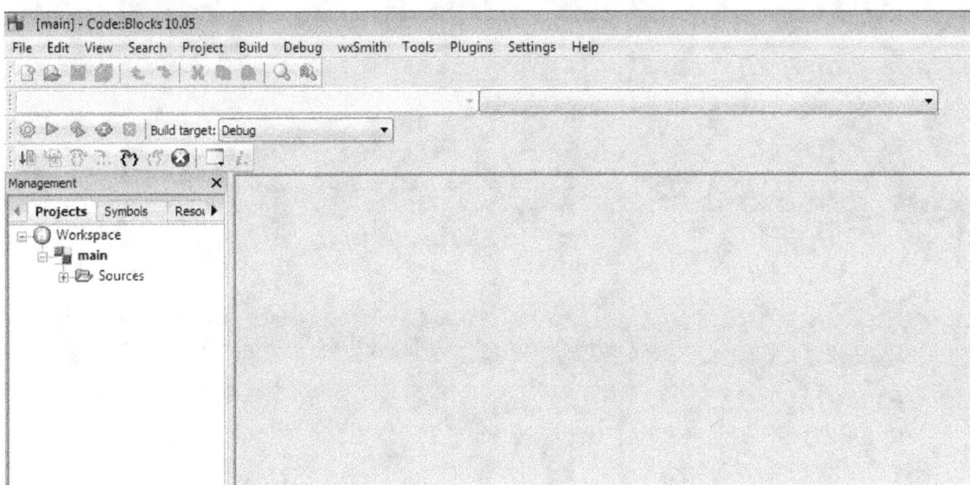

Click on 'source'

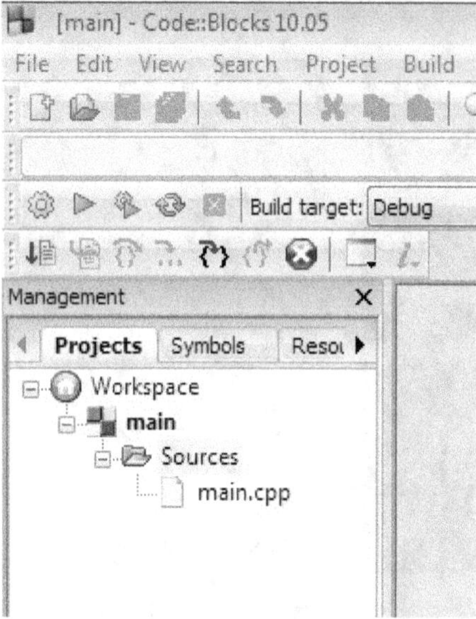

Then click on 'main.cpp', then the main function structure will be created automatically

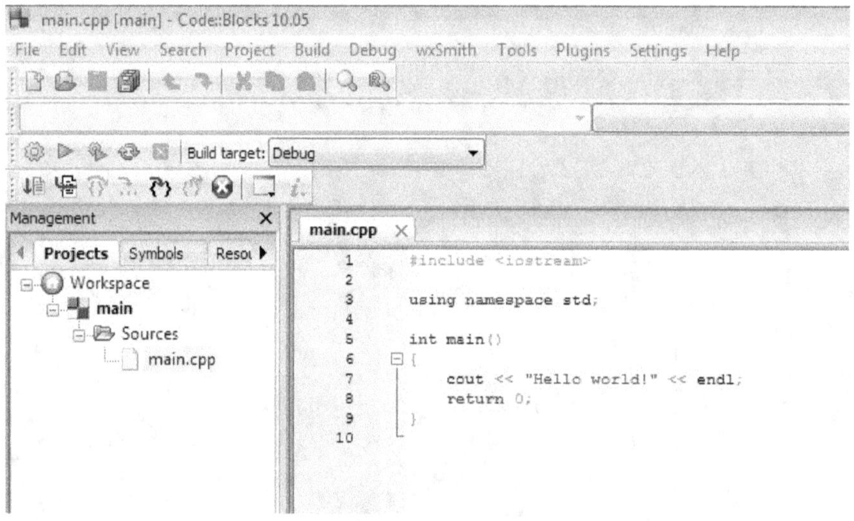

Now, click on 'file'

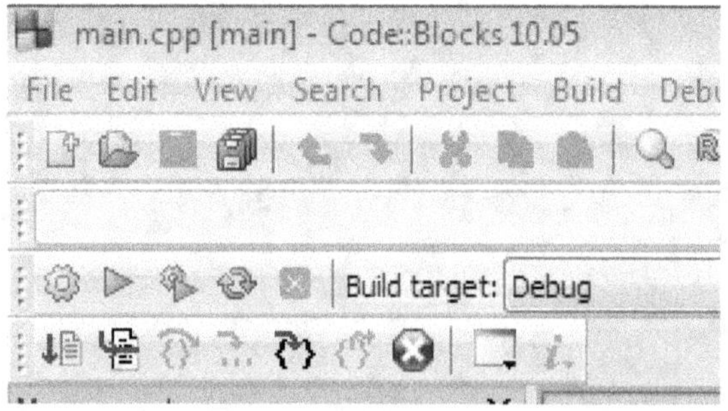

After clicking 'file', go 'new' and then select 'class'

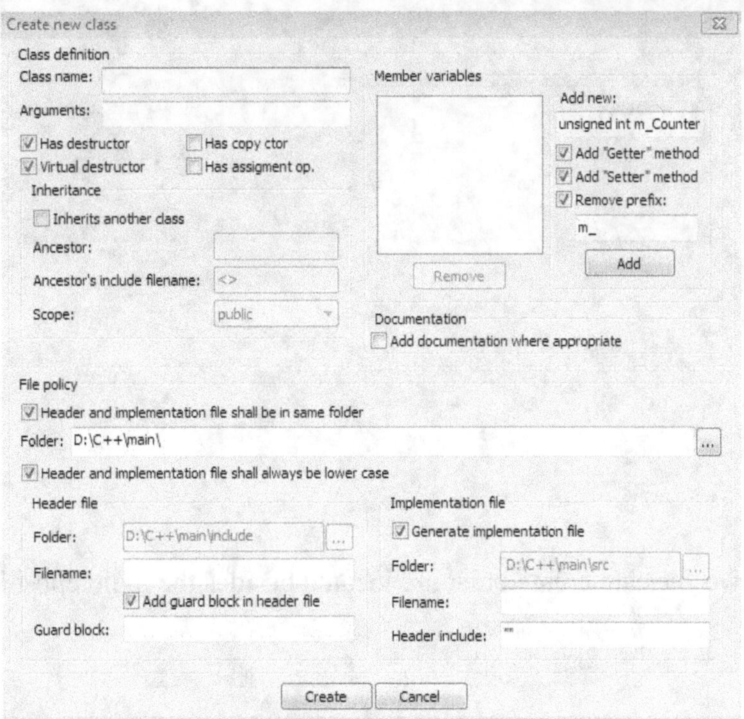

Give class name and deselect the 'has destructor'

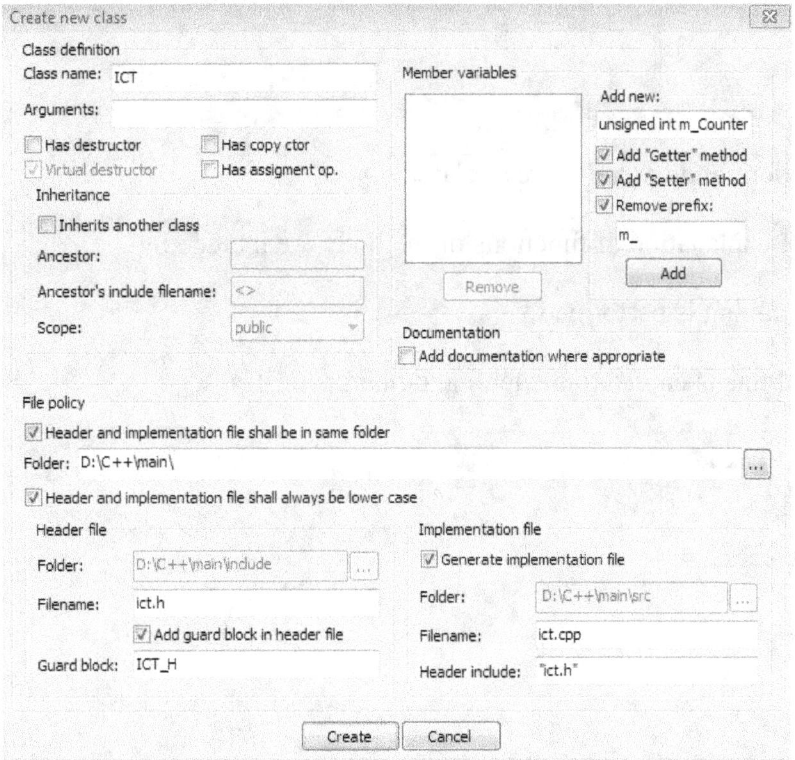

Then click 'create'

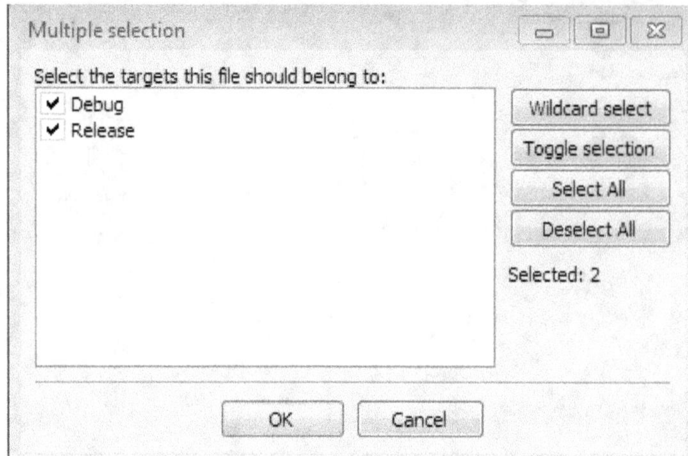

Click 'ok'

Now additionally two files are created that are located besides the main.cpp file

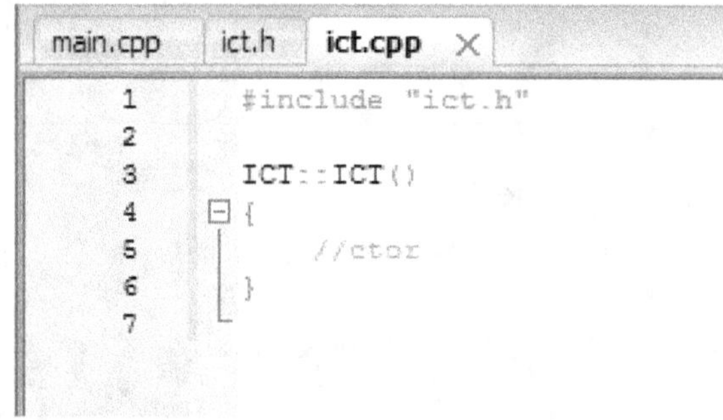

In ict.h file, functions and variables are declared

In ict.cpp file, the explanation of functions or the body are included.

In main.cpp file, calling is performed.

Now, the selected line is copied to the ict.h and main.cpp files

```
main.cpp    *ict.h  ×  ict.cpp
 1      #ifndef ICT_H
 2      #define ICT_H
 3
 4
 5      class ICT
 6    {
 7        public:
 8            ICT();
 9        protected:
10        private:
11    };
12
13    #endif // ICT_H
14
```

```
main.cpp    *ict.h  ×  ict.cpp
 1      #ifndef ICT_H
 2      #define ICT_H
 3      #include "ict.h"
 4
 5      class ICT
 6    {
 7        public:
 8            ICT();
 9        protected:
10        private:
11    };
12
13    #endif // ICT_H
14
```

```
*main.cpp  ×  ict.h  ict.cpp
 1      #include <iostream>
 2      #include "ict.h"
 3      using namespace std;
 4
 5      int main()
 6    {
```

Problem-37(b): How to declare a constructor using separate files?

main.cpp	ict.h	ict.cpp

``cpp
#include <iostream>
#include<conio.h>
#include "ict.h"
using namespace std;
 	
int main()
{
   ICT c;
   getch();
}
``
	``cpp
	#ifndef ICT_H
	#define ICT_H
	#include "ict.h"
	
	class ICT
	{
	   public:
	     ICT();
	   protected:
	   private:
	};
	
	#endif // ICT_H
	``
		``cpp
		#include<iostream>
		#include "ict.h"
		using namespace std;
		
		ICT::ICT()
		{
		   cout<<"Constructor is
		called.";
		}
		``

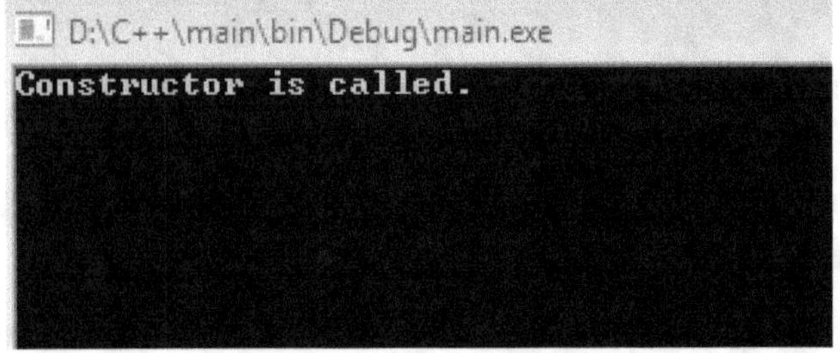

Problem-37(c): How to declare a constructor and function in separate files.

main.cpp	ict.h	ict.cpp

``cpp
#include <iostream>
#include<conio.h>
#include "ict.h"
using namespace std;
 	
int main()
{
   ICT c;
   c.display();
   getch();
}
``
	``cpp
	#ifndef ICT_H
	#define ICT_H
	#include "ict.h"
	
	class ICT
	{
	   public:
	     ICT();
	     void display();//body is
	implemented in the ict.cpp file
	   protected:
	   private:
	};
	
	#endif // ICT_H
	``
		``cpp
		#include<iostream>
		#include "ict.h"
		using namespace std;
		
		ICT::ICT()
		{
		   cout<<"Constructor is
		called."<<endl;
		}
		void ICT::display()
		{
		   cout<<"Display function is
		called.";
		}
		``

Problem-37(d): How to declare a constructor and destructor in separate files.

At first, 'has destructor' must be enabled.

main.cpp	ict.h	ict.cpp

``cpp
#include <iostream>
#include "ict.h"
using namespace std;
 	
int main()
{
   ICT c;
   return 0;
}
``
	``cpp
	#ifndef ICT_H
	#define ICT_H
	#include "ict.h"
	
	class ICT
	{
	   public:
	      ICT();//Constructor is declared
	      ~ICT();//Destructor is declared
	   protected:
	   private:
	};
	
	#endif // ICT_H
	``
		``cpp
		#include "ict.h"
		#include <iostream>
		using namespace std;
		ICT::ICT()//body of constructor
		{
		   cout<<"Constructor is called."<<endl;
		}
		
		ICT::~ICT()//body of destructor
		{
		   cout<<"Destructor is called."<<endl;
		}
		``

```
D:\C++\main\bin\Debug\main.exe

Constructor is called.
Destructor is called.

Process returned 0 (0x0)   execution time : 0.040 s
Press any key to continue.
```

Problem-37(e): How to declare constructor, function and destructor in separate files.

main.cpp	ict.h	ict.cpp
```#include <iostream>``` ``#include "ict.h"`` ``using namespace std;`` ``int main()`` ``{`` ``ICT c;`` ``c.display();`` ``return 0;`` ``}``	``#ifndef ICT_H`` ``#define ICT_H`` ``#include "ict.h"`` ``class ICT`` ``{`` ``public:`` ``ICT();//Constructor is declared`` ``~ICT();//Destructor is declared`` ``void display();`` ``protected:`` ``private:`` ``};`` ``#endif // ICT_H``	``#include "ict.h"`` ``#include <iostream>`` ``using namespace std;`` ``ICT::ICT()//body of constructor`` ``{`` ``cout<<"Constructor is called."<<endl;`` ``}`` ``ICT::~ICT()//body of destructor`` ``{`` ``cout<<"Destructor is called."<<endl;`` ``}`` ``void ICT::display()`` ``{`` ``cout<<"Display is called."<<endl;`` ``}``

```
D:\C++\main\bin\Debug\main.exe
Constructor is called.
Display is called.
Destructor is called.

Process returned 0 (0x0)   execution time : 0.720 s
Press any key to continue.
```

8.6 Selection Operator

Problem-38: Write a C++ program to call a function located inside a class using pointer with selection operator.

main.cpp	ict.h	ict.cpp
``#include <iostream>`` ``#include "ict.h"`` ``using namespace std;`` ``int main()`` ``{`` ``ICT c;`` ``ICT *p=&c;`` ``p->display();`` ``return 0;``	``#ifndef ICT_H`` ``#define ICT_H`` ``#include "ict.h"`` ``class ICT`` ``{`` ``public:`` ``ICT();//Constructor is declared`` ``~ICT();//Destructor is``	``#include "ict.h"`` ``#include <iostream>`` ``using namespace std;`` ``ICT::ICT()//body of constructor`` ``{`` ``cout<<"Constructor is called."<<endl;`` ``}``

`}`	declared
	    void display();
	  protected:
	  private:
	`};`
	
	#endif // ICT_H
		ICT::~ICT()//body of
		destructor
		`{`
		   cout<<"Destructor is
		called."<<endl;
		`}`
		
		void ICT::display()
		`{`
		   cout<<"Display is
		called."<<endl;
		`}`

```
D:\C++\main\bin\Debug\main.exe
Constructor is called.
Display is called.
Destructor is called.

Process returned 0 (0x0)    execution time : 0.040 s
Press any key to continue.
```

8.7 Member Initializer list/ Constructor Initializer

Problem-39(a): Write a C++ program to create a constructor named 'student' to pass and print a value named 'admissionFee' through it after creating object named 'rahim'.

```cpp
#include <iostream>

#include<conio.h>

using namespace std;

class student

{

    public:

    int admissionFee;

    student(int x)

    {

        admissionFee=x;
```

```cpp
    cout<<admissionFee<<endl;

  }

};

int main()

{

  student rahim(15000);

  getch();

}
```

```
D:\C++\const\bin\Debug\const.exe
15000
```

Problem-39(b): Write a C++ program to create a constructor named 'student' to pass and print a constant value named 'admissionFee' through it after creating object named 'rahim'.

```cpp
#include <iostream>

#include<conio.h>

using namespace std;

class student

{

  public:

  const int admissionFee;//it shows error, beacuse value has to be imported instantly with declaring const

  student(int x)

  :admissionFee(x)//error can be solved using member or constructor initialization
```

```cpp
    {
        cout<<admissionFee<<endl;
    }
};
int main()
{
    student rahim(15000);
    getch();
}
```


Problem-39(c): Write a C++ program to create a constructor named 'student' to pass and print two constant values named 'admissionFee' & 'examFee' through it after creating object named 'rahim'.

```cpp
#include <iostream>
#include<conio.h>
using namespace std;
class student
{
    public:
    const int admissionFee;
    const int examFee;
    student(int x,int y)
    :admissionFee(x),examFee(y)
```

```cpp
    {
        cout<<"Admission Fee is: "<<admissionFee<<endl;

        cout<<"Exam Fee is: "<<examFee<<endl;

    }

};

int main()

{

    student rahim(15000,500);

    getch();

}
```

Problem-39(d): Write a C++ program to create a constructor named 'student' to pass and print two constant values named 'admissionFee' & 'examFee' and one non-constant value named 'ID' through it after creating object named 'rahim'.

```cpp
#include <iostream>

#include<conio.h>

using namespace std;

class student

{

    public:

    const int admissionFee;

    const int examFee;

    int ID;

    student(int x,int y,int z)
```

```cpp
:admissionFee(x),examFee(y)

{

    ID=z;

    cout<<"ID is: "<<ID<<endl;

    cout<<"Admission Fee is: "<<admissionFee<<endl;

    cout<<"Exam Fee is: "<<examFee<<endl;

}
};
int main()
{

  student rahim(15000,500,101);

  getch();

}
```

8.8 Encapsulation

Problem-40(a): Write a C++ program to implement the feature of Object Oriented Programming called encapsulation.

(i)   Combining variables & functions:

```cpp
#include <iostream>

#include<string>

using namespace std;

class student

{

    public:

    int id;

    string name;

    void display()

    {

        cout<<id<<" "<<name<<endl;

    }

};

int main()

{

    student boy;

    boy.id=101;

    boy.name="rahim";

    boy.display();

    return 0;

}
```

(ii)   *Protecting data by declaring them as private:*

```cpp
#include <iostream>
#include<string>
using namespace std;
class student
{
    private:
    int id;
    string name;
    public:
    void display()
    {
        cout<<id<<" "<<name<<endl;
    }
};
int main()
{
    student boy;
    boy.id=101;
    boy.name="rahim";
    boy.display();
    return 0;
}
```

Logs & others

| Code::Blocks | Search results | Build log | Build messages × | Debugger |

File	Line	Message
		=== encap, Debug ===
D:\C++\encap\m...		In function 'int main()':
D:\C++\encap\m...	7	error: 'int student::id' is private
D:\C++\encap\m...	18	error: within this context
D:\C++\encap\m...	8	error: 'std::string student::name' is private

#include <iostream>

#include<string>

using namespace std;

class student

{

```cpp
private:

int id;

string name;

public:

void display()

{

    cout<<"Private data ID & Name will be hiddden from other classes."<<endl;

    cout<<"They can only be accessed through public function of their current class."<<endl;

}

};

int main()

{

    student boy;

    boy.display();

    return 0;

}
```

Problem-40(b): Write a C++ program to get access of the private data using setter function & getter function.

```cpp
#include <iostream>

#include<string>

using namespace std;

class student

{
```

```cpp
private:

string name;

public:

void setName(string x)

{

  name=x;

}

string getName()

{

  return name;

}

};

int main()

{

  student boy;

  boy.setName("rahim");

  cout<<boy.getName();

  return 0;

}
```

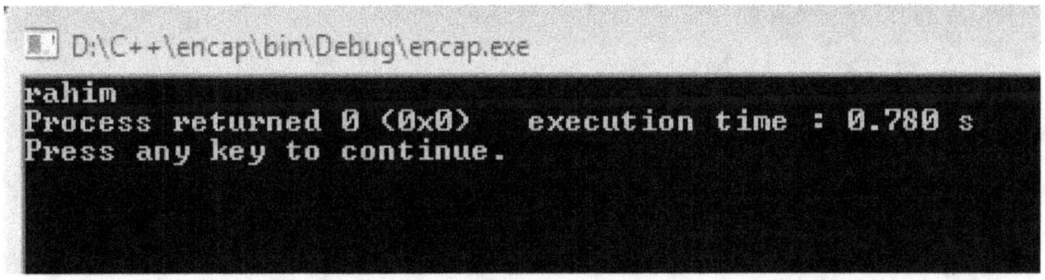

Problem-40(c): Write a C++ program to get the sum of two numbers only. User is restricted to access the number of input variables.

```cpp
#include <iostream>

#include<conio.h>

using namespace std;

class sum

{

    private:

    int a,b,c;

    public:

    void display()

    {

        cout<<"Enter two numbers: "<<endl;

        cin>>a>>b;

        c=a+b;

        cout<<"Sum is "<<c;

    }

};

int main()

{

    sum s ;

    s.display();

    getch();

}
```

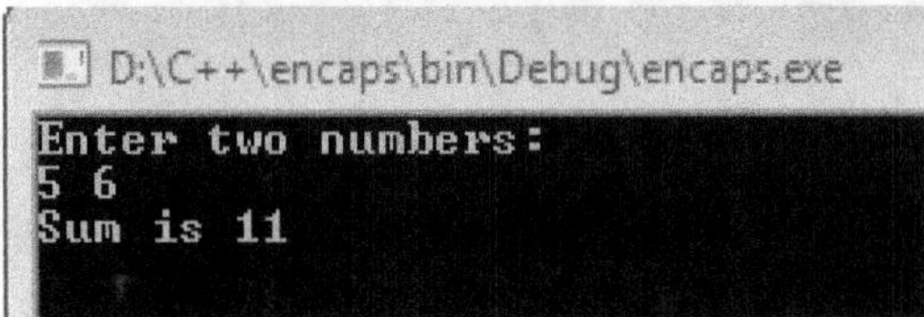

8.9 this keyword

Problem-41: Write a C++ program to convert the name of local variable as like as the name of class variable using the 'this' keyword.

```cpp
#include <iostream>

#include<string>

using namespace std;

class student

{

    public:

    string name;

    student(string x)

    {

        name=x;

    }

    void display()

    {

        cout<<name<<endl;

    }

};

int main()

{

    student boy("rahim");
```

```
    boy.display();

    return 0;

}
```

D:\C++\encap\bin\Debug\encap.exe

rahim

Here, name is class variable and x is local variable. If we want to keep the local variable as same as class variable, this keyword will be used.

```cpp
#include <iostream>

#include<string>

using namespace std;

class student

{

    public:

    string name;

    student(string name)

    {

        this-> name=name;

    }

    void display()

    {

        cout<<name<<endl;

    }

};

int main()

{
```

```cpp
student boy("rahim");

boy.display();

return 0;

}
```


8.10 Inheritance

Problem-42(a): Write a C++ program to implement inheritance feature of object oriented programming language. At first create a person class, then inherits the person class by student class to avoid the same functions of same attributes containing both in person class & student class.

```cpp
#include <iostream>

using namespace std;

class person

{

    public:

    int id;

    string name;

    void display1()

    {

        cout<<id<<" "<<name<<endl;

    }

};

class student:public person
```

```cpp
{
    public:
    int age;
    void display2()
    {
        display1();
        cout<<"The age of karim is: "<<age;
    }
};
int main()
{
    student r,k;
    r.id=101;
    r.name="rahim";
    r.display1();
    k.age=25;
    k.id=102;
    k.name="karim";
    k.display2();
    return 0;
}
```

```
D:\C++\inherit\bin\Debug\inherit.exe
101 rahim
102 karim
The age of karim is: 25
```

Problem-42(b): Write a C++ program to create game characters using the concept of inheritance.

```cpp
#include <iostream>

using namespace std;

   class Person
   {
      public:
         string profession;

         int age;

         void display()
         {
            cout << "My profession is: " << profession << endl;

            cout << "My age is: " << age << endl;

            walk();

            talk();
         }
         void walk()
         {
            cout << "I can walk." << endl;
         }
         void talk()
         {
            cout << "I can talk." << endl;
         }
   };
```

```cpp
// MathsTeacher class is derived from base class Person.

class MathsTeacher : public Person
{
  public:
    void teachMaths()
    {
       cout << "I can teach Maths." << endl;
    }
};

// Footballer class is derived from base class Person.

class Footballer : public Person
{
  public:
  void playFootball()
  {
     cout << "I can play Football." << endl;
  }
};

int main()
{
    MathsTeacher teacher;

    teacher.profession = "Teacher";

    teacher.age = 23;

    teacher.display();

    teacher.teachMaths();
```

```
        Footballer footballer;

        footballer.profession = "Footballer";

        footballer.age = 19;

        footballer.display();

        footballer.playFootball();

        return 0;

    }
```


8.10.1 Inheritance Types

Problem-43(a): Write a C++ program to find the product of two numbers chosen by user using the concept of single inheritance.

```cpp
class A    // base class
{
    ..........
};
class B : acess_specifier A    // derived class
{
    ...........
} ;
```

#include <iostream>

using namespace std;

class base   //single base class

{

  public:

    int x;

```cpp
void getdata()

{

cout << "Enter the value of x = ";

cin >> x;

}

};

class derive : public base    //single derived class

{

  private:

   int y;

  public:

  void readdata()

  {

   cout << "Enter the value of y = ";

   cin >> y;

  }

  void product()

  {

   cout << "Product = " << x * y;

  }

};


int main()

{

   derive a;     //object of derived class
```

```
    a.getdata();

    a.readdata();

    a.product();

    return 0;

}       //end of program
```

```
D:\C++\inherit\bin\Debug\inherit.exe
Enter the value of x = 2
Enter the value of y = 3
Product = 6
```

Problem-43(b): Write a C++ program to find the product of three numbers chosen by user using the concept of multilevel inheritance.

```
class A // base class
{
    ...........
};
class B : acess_specifier A // derived class
{
    ...........
 } ;
 class C : access_specifier B // derived from derived class B
 {
    ...........
 } ;
```

```
#include <iostream>

using namespace std;

class base //single base class

{

        public:

        int x;

        void getdata()

        {

        cout << "Enter value of x= "<<endl;
```

```cpp
        cin >> x;

    }

};

class derive1 : public base // derived class from base class

{

        public:

        int y;

        void readdata()

        {

            cout << "Enter value of y= "<<endl;

            cin >> y;

        }

};

class derive2 : public derive1   // derived from class derive1

{

        private:

        int z;

        public:

        void indata()

        {

        cout << "Enter value of z= "<<endl;

        cin >> z;

        }

        void product()

        {
```

```cpp
        cout << "Product= " << x * y * z;

    }

};

int main()

{

    derive2 a;     //object of derived class

    a.getdata();

    a.readdata();

    a.indata();

    a.product();

    return 0;

}                //end of program
```

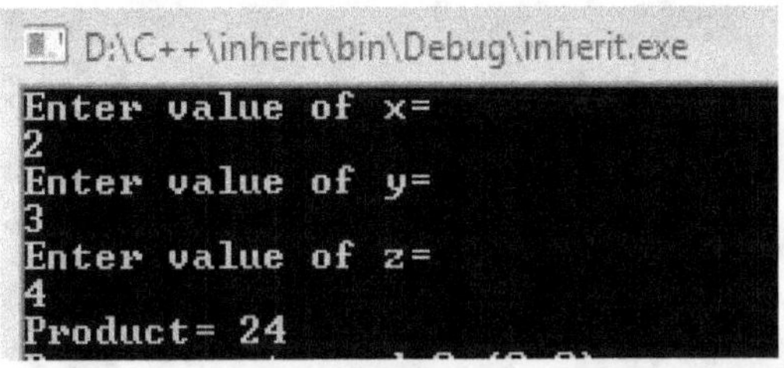

```
D:\C++\inherit\bin\Debug\inherit.exe
Enter value of x=
2
Enter value of y=
3
Enter value of z=
4
Product= 24
```

Problem-43(c): Write a C++ program to find the product and sum of two numbers chosen by user using the concept of hierarchical inheritance.

```cpp
class A // base class
{
    ..............
};
class B : access_specifier A // derived class from A
{
    ...........
} ;
class C : access_specifier A // derived class from A
{
    ...........
} ;
class D : access_specifier A // derived class from A
{
    ...........
} ;
```

```cpp
#include <iostream>

using namespace std;

class A //single base class

{

    public:

        int x, y;

        void getdata()

        {

            cout << "Enter value of x and y: "<<endl;

            cin >> x >> y;

        }

};

class B : public A //B is derived from class base

{

    public:

        void product()

        {

            cout << "Product= " << x * y<<endl;

        }

};

class C : public A //C is also derived from class base

{

    public:

        void sum()
```

```cpp
    {

    cout << "Sum= " << x + y<<endl;

    }

};

int main()

{

    B obj1;        //object of derived class B

    C obj2;        //object of derived class C

    obj1.getdata();

    obj1.product();

    obj2.getdata();

    obj2.sum();

    return 0;

} //end of program
```

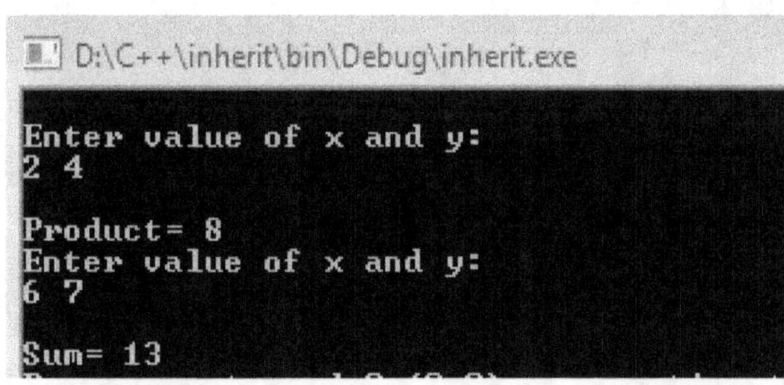

Problem-43(d): Write a C++ program to find the sum of two numbers using the concept of hybrid inheritance.

```cpp
class A
{
    .........
};
class B : public A
{
    ..........
} ;
class C
{
```

```cpp
          . . . . . . . . . .
};
 class D : public B, public C
{
          . . . . . . . . . .
};
```

#include <iostream>

using namespace std;

class A

{

        public:

        int x;

};

class B : public A

{

        public:

        B()   //constructor to initialize x in base class A

        {

          x = 10;

        }

};

class C

{

        public:

        int y;

        C()   //constructor to initialize y

        {

```cpp
        y = 4;


    }
};
class D : public B, public C   //D is derived from class B and class C
{
        public:
        void sum()
        {
           cout << "Sum= " << x + y;
        }
};


int main()
{
D obj1;        //object of derived class D
obj1.sum();
return 0;
}                //end of program
```

```
D:\C++\inherit\bin\Debug\inherit.exe
Sum= 14
```

Problem-43(e): Write a C++ program to find the sum of two numbers chosen by user using the concept of multiple inheritance.

```
class A
{
  . . . . . . . . . .
};
class B
{
  . . . . . . . . . . .
  } ;
class C : acess_specifier A,access_specifier A // derived class from A and B
{
  . . . . . . . . . . .
  } ;
```

#include<iostream>

using namespace std;

class A

{

       public:

       int x;

       void getx()

  {

      cout << "enter value of x: "<<endl;

      cin >> x;

  }

};

class B

{

       public:

       int y;

       void gety()

```cpp
    {

        cout << "enter value of y: "<<endl;

        cin >> y;

    }

};

class C : public A, public B   //C is derived from class A and class B

{

        public:

        void sum()

        {

            cout << "Sum = " << x + y;

        }

};


int main()

{

        C obj1; //object of derived class C

        obj1.getx();

        obj1.gety();

        obj1.sum();

        return 0;

}       //end of program
```

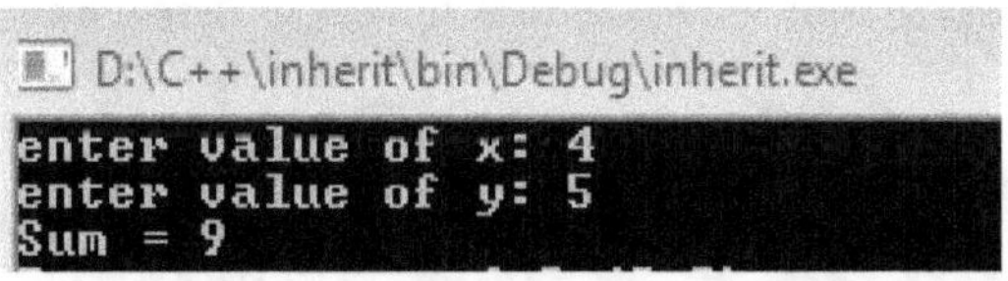

8.11 Function Overriding

Problem-44: Write a C++ program to implement the function overriding.

```cpp
#include <iostream>
#include<conio.h>
using namespace std;
class person
{
   public:
   void display()
   {
     cout<<"I am a person"<<endl;
   }
};
class student:public person
{
   public:
   void display()
   {
     cout<<"I am a student"<<endl;
   }
};
class teacher:public student
{
   public:
   void display()
```

```cpp
    {
        cout<<"I am a teacher"<<endl;
    }
};
int main()
{
    person p;
    p.display();
    student s;
    s.display();
    teacher t;
    t.display();
    getch();
}
```

8.12 Polymorphism

Problem-45: Write a C++ program to realize the feature of object oriented programming called polymorphism.

```cpp
#include <iostream>

#include<conio.h>

using namespace std;

class person

{

    public:

    void display()

    {

        cout<<"I am a person"<<endl;

    }

};

class student:public person

{

    public:

    void display()

    {

        cout<<"I am a student"<<endl;

    }

};

class teacher: public person

{

    public:
```

```cpp
    void display()

    {

        cout<<"I am a teacher"<<endl;

    }

};

int main()

{

    teacher t;

    student s;

    person p;

    p.display();

    s.display();

    t.display();

    getch();

}
```

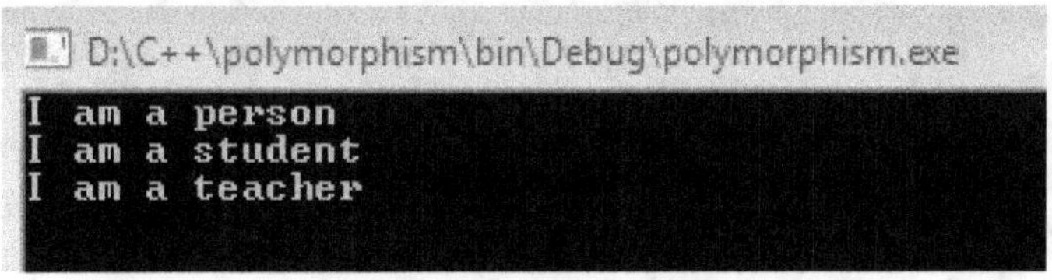

8.13 Virtual Function

Problem-46: Write a C++ program to realize the feature of object oriented programming called polymorphism by creating a pointer.

```cpp
#include <iostream>
#include<conio.h>
using namespace std;
class person
{
    public:
    void display()
    {
        cout<<"I am a person"<<endl;
    }
};
class student:public person
{
    public:
    void display()
    {
        cout<<"I am a student"<<endl;
    }
};
class teacher: public person
{
    public:
```

```cpp
void display()

{

    cout<<"I am a teacher"<<endl;

}

};

int main()

{

    teacher t;

    student s;

    person *p;

    p=&s;

    p->display();

    getch();

}
```


But the desired output was, 'I am a student'. Why? Because, we did not use virtual function. We want to make person class as a virtual function, so that every class can work with the function of person class.

```cpp
#include <iostream>

#include<conio.h>

using namespace std;

class person

{

    public:
```

```cpp
virtual void display()

{

cout<<"I am a person"<<endl;

}

};

class student:public person

{

public:

void display()

{

cout<<"I am a student"<<endl;

}

};

class teacher: public person

{

public:

void display()

{

cout<<"I am a teacher"<<endl;

}

};

int main()

{

teacher t;

student s;
```

```cpp
person *p;

p=&s;

p->display();

getch();

}
```



```cpp
#include <iostream>

#include<conio.h>

using namespace std;

class person

{

    public:

    virtual void display()

    {

        cout<<"I am a person"<<endl;

    }

};

class student:public person

{

    public:

    void display()

    {

        cout<<"I am a student"<<endl;
```

```cpp
    }
};
class teacher: public person
{
  public:
  void display()
  {
    cout<<"I am a teacher"<<endl;
  }
};
int main()
{
  teacher t;
  student s;
  person *p;
  p=&s;
  p->display();
  p=&t;
  p->display();
  getch();
}
```

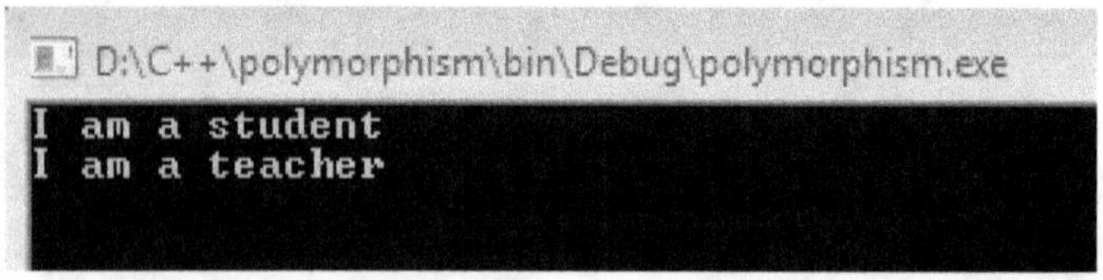

8.14 Abstraction

Problem-47: Write a C++ program to realize the feature of object oriented programming called Abstraction by creating abstract class.

```cpp
#include <iostream>

#include<conio.h>

using namespace std;

class MobileUser   //abstract class declaration

{

   public:

   void call()   //we can declare non virtual function of abstract class

   {

     cout<<"Hello"<<endl;

   }

   virtual void SendMessage()=0; //Pure virtual function with no body

};

//Inheritance

class Rahim : public MobileUser

{

   public:

   void SendMessage() // 5 number Property of abstract class

   {

     cout<<"This is Rahim"<<endl;

   }

};

class Karim : public MobileUser
```

```cpp
{
  public:
  void SendMessage()
  {
    cout<<"This is Karim."<<endl;
  }
};
int main()
{
    MobileUser *m; // 2 number property of abstract class
    Rahim r;
    Karim k;
    m=&r;
    m->SendMessage();
    m=&k;
    m->SendMessage();
    getch();
}
```

```
D:\C++\abstraction\bin\Debug\abstraction.exe
This is Rahim
This is Karim.
```

```cpp
#include <iostream>
#include<conio.h>
using namespace std;
class MobileUser   //abstract class declaration
```

```cpp
{
    public:
    void call()   //we can declare non virtual function of abstract class
    {
        cout<<"Hello"<<endl;
    }
    virtual void SendMessage()=0; //Pure virtual function with no body
};
//Inheritance
class Rahim : public MobileUser
{
    public:
    void SendMessage() // 5 number Property of abstract class
    {
        cout<<"This is Rahim"<<endl;
    }
};
class Karim : public MobileUser
{
    public:
    void SendMessage()
    {
        cout<<"This is Karim."<<endl;
    }
};
```

```cpp
int main()
{

    MobileUser *m; // 2 number property of abstract class

    Rahim r;

    Karim k;

    m->call();

    m=&r;

    m->SendMessage();

    m=&k;

    m->SendMessage();

    getch();

}
```

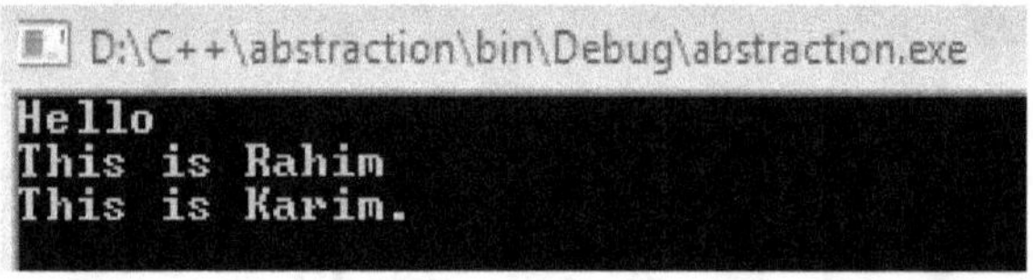

```
D:\C++\abstraction\bin\Debug\abstraction.exe
Hello
This is Rahim
This is Karim.
```